CW01456838

Greenfinches

Peter Lander and Bob Partridge

Bird photography by Dennis Avon, MIOP, ARPS

Greenfinches

Peter Lander and Bob Partridge

KINGDOM

© Kingdom Books 1998. All rights reserved. No part of this publication may be reproduced, stored in a retrieval system, or transmitted in any form or by any means, electronic, mechanical, photocopying, recording or otherwise, without the written permission of the publisher.

Published by Kingdom Books
PO Box 15
Waterlooville PO7 6BQ
England

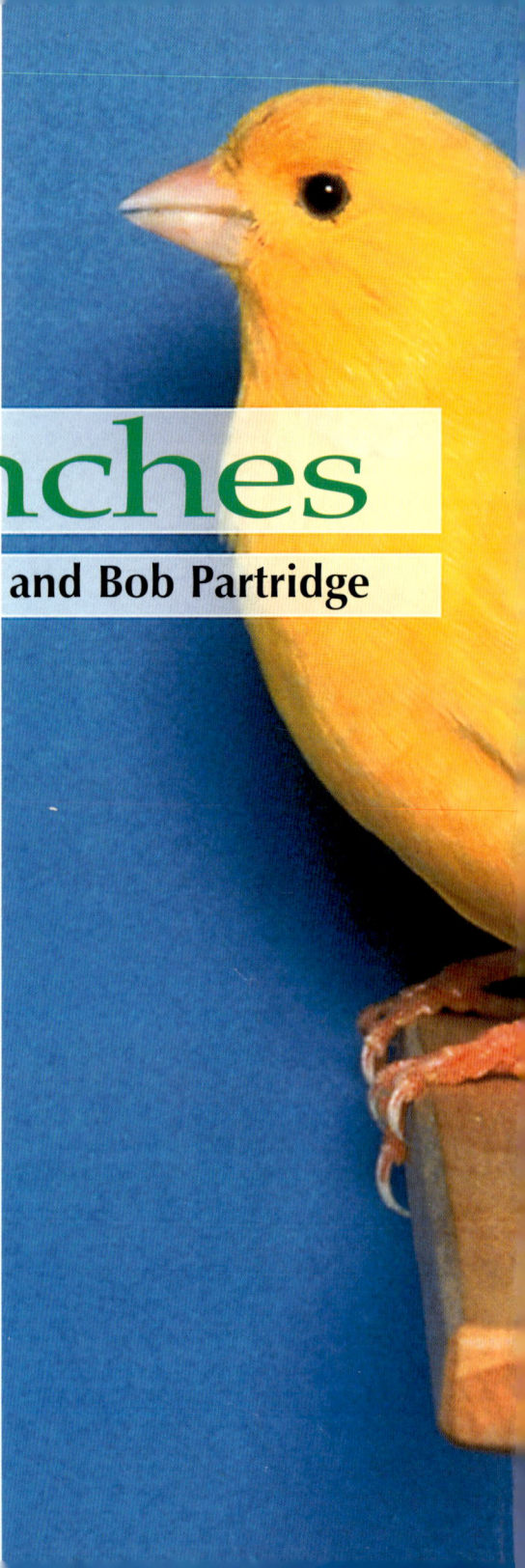

Contents

Preface

This book is the first in a series intended as a follow-on to the very successful book *British Birds in Aviculture*, published in conjunction with the British Bird Council. By concentrating on no more than three species in each book we can treat them in much greater depth. It also enables us to update the original book where necessary in the light of the latest knowledge and experience.

Our old friend the late Walter Lewis always used to say, 'The golden rule in bird breeding is that there is no golden rule.' By this he meant that there are always exceptions in anything to do with birds, and the experience of one successful breeder is totally different to that of another, for no apparent reason. Walter was considered to be one of the most knowledgeable British fanciers of his time in the field of British birds, mules and hybrids.

All we can do is pass on our knowledge and experience as a basis on which each breeder can develop his or her own system. As joint authors we can sometimes give different information, hopefully making this book all the more interesting and useful.

Peter Lander and Bob Partridge

Popular British Birds in Aviculture series:

No 1: Greenfinches   *No 2: Siskins and Goldfinches*

No 3: Redpolls, Twites and Linnets   *No 4: Bullfinches, Chaffinches and Bramblings*

Cages and Aviaries

Before obtaining any birds it is essential to have suitable accommodation. While this need be neither expensive nor ornamental, it must be suitable for the birds' needs. They must have room to move about freely, shelter from the elements and protection from such enemies as cats, owls, weasels, rats and other vermin. There must also be sufficient food and water receptacles.

Birds certainly look nicer in an aviary but, for enthusiasts who have neither the space nor the means, adequate accommodation can be provided in cages. These can be situated in a shed in the garden. However, many sheds need extra windows to allow the birds enough light to feed throughout the day; if the shed is dark they will spend a great deal of time roosting. There must be good ventilation, allowing continuous free passage of air. Heating is not necessary for temperate-zone birds normally resident in this country throughout the year. On the other hand, it is essential that the birds can drink at all times during the day and, unless the fancier is at home all day, the shed should be heated or insulated sufficiently to prevent the water from freezing during severe weather. A study of the advertisements in the fancy press will produce information on sheds in a variety of shapes and sizes, all designed for bird keeping.

Birds need room if they are to breed - in fact the larger the cage the better. The minimum size recommended is 91cm x 60cm x 46cm (36in x 24in x 18in), containing only one pair. Far better results will be obtained by having a few pairs in large cages than by having more pairs in smaller cages. Natural branches can be fixed in the cages for perches; these look nicer and are much more comfortable for the birds' feet than the round doweling often used. Do not overcrowd the cage with these as flying space is essential. In one end of the cage fix a bunch of conifer or other suitable evergreen, with a forked branch in the middle to support a nest. Alternatively, a small wicker basket or half-open-fronted, open-topped box can be used (fig 1). The object is to provide privacy and a feeling of security for the sitting hen, but the bunch must not be thick enough to exclude too much light or prevent the birds from entering easily: just enough to give the necessary seclusion.

Contrary to advice frequently given, the most consistent results are obtained in sheds and aviaries facing east. This is because birds, particularly when nesting, do not like being

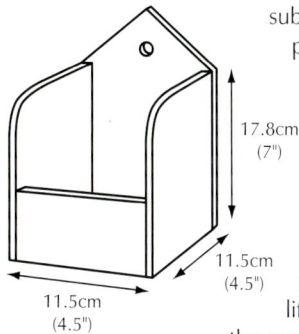

17.8cm
(7")

11.5cm
(4.5")

11.5cm
(4.5")

Fig 1: Nest box

subjected to the mid-day sun and, in the wild, nearly always choose a shaded position. They also like protection from the prevailing west winds and, in the wild, choose a situation that is protected in this respect also. It is not always possible to provide the ideal so it is advisable to fix up some means of providing shade and protection.

The only real disadvantage to cage breeding is the extra work involved in providing a sufficient variety of foods on which the birds can feed their young, particularly when they are first hatched. Even in a small aviary it is much easier to provide a variety, and the birds will find a few insects to supplement their diet, which can be so beneficial in the early stages of a chick's life. To some extent this can be overcome if the birds can be persuaded to feed the young ones on egg food. More details on feeding are given in chapter 5.

It is not essential to provide near-natural conditions to breed our popular native birds. The majority of these common species can be reproduced with the minimum of cover in a small flight. Even a large cage will suffice for many of the hardbills.

Some years ago breeders used large amounts of cover in the form of gorse, broom, conifers and other evergreens but nowadays the birds are much more domesticated and breed very successfully with only a minimum of cover. This has the added benefit of allowing the breeder to observe, study and enjoy the birds to a far greater degree.

Aviary Construction

An aviary can be any size but the minimum recommended is 180cm x 60cm x 180cm (6ft x 2ft x 6ft). This will hold approximately six non-breeding birds, but generally only one pair of breeding birds. In a mixed aviary one should allow at least 2.25 cubic metres (80 cubic feet) per pair of birds; much more if possible.

Aviaries can be as simple or as elaborate as one wishes, depending on circumstances and funds available, as long as they meet the requirements of the birds. An example of a cheap and easily-constructed aviary is the one designed some years ago by Mr Hylton Blythe (fig 2), which is made as follows. Roofing laths are driven into the ground at 1m (3ft) intervals and cut off to the required height, with further laths nailed along the top and across from side to side. This enables 1m (3ft) wire netting to be stapled to the laths. There is a small door at one end for access, with a shelf above it for food. A further small door gives access to the shelf so that it is not necessary to enter the aviary to feed the birds. Cover must be provided to keep the seed and shelf dry. The birds also need protection from the wind and rain

Yellow dark greenfinch mule cock

and shade from the sun. This can be achieved by nailing boards all round along the top to a width of about 30cm (12in) and the same along the top of the sides. Roofing felt can be used instead of boards if there is wire netting underneath to support it. If all the timber is treated with creosote or bitumen it will last much longer.

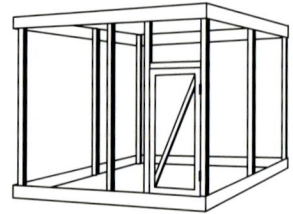

Fig 2: Typical Aviary –
from an original design by Hylton Blythe

Where funds allow, more substantial aviaries give added protection to the birds and last considerably longer. A well-constructed and well-maintained aviary can more than repay the extra expense and labour. For example, solid foundation plinths set well into the ground constructed of 10cm (4in) bricks, blocks or solid concrete 45cm (14in) deep will keep out rats. The base area can then be filled in with earth, pebbles, sand, bark chippings or solid concrete slabs for easy cleaning and disinfecting. Tanalised framing or cedar wood 50mm x 50mm (2in x 2in) will last almost a life time.

Solid timber felted roofs give valuable protection from cats, kestrels, marauding magpies and thunder-storms and also exclude droppings from wild birds, which can pass on disease to the aviary inmates. Solid cladding of the back and at least one third of the sides gives added protection as well as security to the birds (figs 3 and 4).

Large feeding trays can be provided in a completely dry area where they are clear of any perches, thus preventing the birds from eating mouldy or soiled foods. These and many other refinements can be considered for the welfare of the birds, which is paramount if success is to be achieved.

For nesting sites, use small wickerwork baskets with a few twigs tacked around. This gives the birds some degree of privacy. Many birds pick nesting sites completely open to view, despite other more secluded sites being available. Two or three sites should be available to each pair of birds. Provide a little extra cover for any particularly shy specimens. Other acceptable nesting sites are square wooden pans with perforated zinc bottoms. These are used by many breeders of canaries. Canary plastic pans will need to have felt linings glued or sewn inside, but the birds often pull these to pieces, leaving the slippery plastic surface on which they cannot shape a nest. However, a little polyfilla or plaster of Paris wiped

Cinnamon pied greenfinch (hen)

roughly around the inside can be helpful. Plywood or cane strawberry punnets or clay flower pots can also be used. Sites and receptacles will depend on what the birds find acceptable.

Any simple structure with suitably-sized netting will keep birds in, but it is much more difficult to keep vermin out. Some refinements have already been mentioned to overcome this but, if you do not intend to have solid plinths and solid roofs, other methods have to be used. Cats can be a nuisance, especially if they get on the top of an aviary. To overcome this the main frame should be extended about 23cm (9in) and this extension covered with 5cm (2in) netting, often called chicken wire. Cats have difficulty in walking on this netting, and bunches of gorse hung facing downwards on the corner posts will deter them from climbing up.

Rats, if they gain access, will kill the birds and drag them down their holes, so that they all suddenly disappear. This can be overcome by digging a trench round the aviary 30cm (12in) deep and 30cm (12in) wide. The wire netting is extended down the side of the trench and along the bottom in the shape of a letter L. The trench is then filled in.

Mice are much more difficult to exclude. Although they do not kill birds directly, they carry diseases and cause considerable disturbance, jeopardising breeding results. Also, where mice can get in, weasels will follow, and they kill and eat every bird in sight in no time at all. Mice and weasels can get through 1.3cm (0.5in) netting, which is generally used for aviaries: 1cm (0.4in)

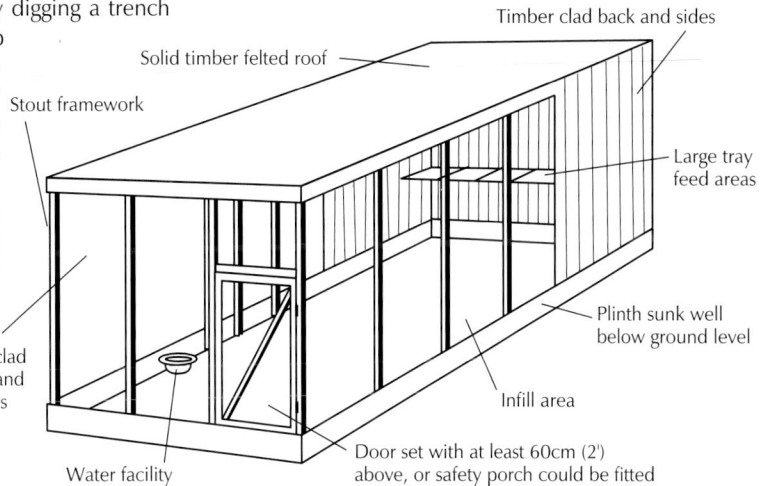

Fig 3: A well constructed aviary 1.8m x 3.6m x 1.8m (6ft x 12ft x 6ft) would accommodate 4 mixed pairs or up to 20 non-breeding birds

netting, which is much more expensive, will keep out all but baby mice. It is therefore very important to keep a sharp look out and take quick action if any signs of mice are seen by setting traps and putting down poison. Both traps and poison must be suitably protected from pets and children, especially as they generally cannot be placed inside the aviary. There are now, however, some traps which catch the mice alive and which can be used inside an aviary safely.

A small aviary for each pair of birds is considered ideal, especially if it is your intention to specialise in a particular species. On the other hand, large aviaries containing several species, such as pairs of redpolls, siskins, linnets, twites and goldfinches, will prove perfectly satisfactory. Greenfinches can usually be trusted with these smaller finches throughout the year. They can also be housed with finches of their own size, such as bullfinches, chaffinches, bramblings or buntings, outside the breeding season, though mixing these species is not recommended during the breeding season. Housing of all species needs careful consideration to suit individual needs.

Trouble can be experienced when just two pairs of different species are kept and bred in one aviary, because one pair will sometimes chase the other continually, preventing feeding. To have either one pair or three or more pairs in a flight usually prevents trouble, but always provide one large feeding area or several smaller ones.

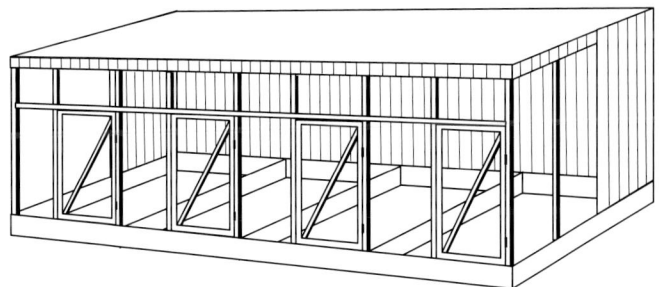

Fig 4: A similar sized aviary partitioned to take 4 segregated breeding pairs; a front corridor could be added for safety

Isolated Type of Nesting Site

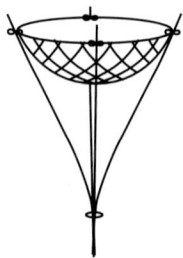

a: Basket wired to stout twigs

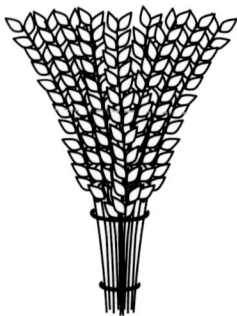

b: Surrounded by evergreen twigs and wire-tied

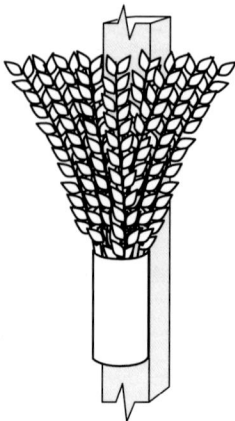

c: Finished nesting site inserted in down-pipe which has been fixed to framework

Fig 5: Nesting sites

The pros and cons of different materials for the floor area, touched on earlier, are governed by the conditions and needs of both the birds and the keeper. Earth is the natural floor covering and, provided that overstocking is avoided, the birds can derive much benefit in the form of trace elements from the soil. Waste seeds which germinate are a welcome addition to the birds' diet. The vegetation attracts a myriad of insect life, which again is very beneficial, especially when young are being reared. The drawback is that it is difficult to prevent mice from burrowing in and breeding in the aviary, contaminating both the food and the soil. Earth floors are also difficult to disinfect and keep clean. Liming annually will help to keep it sweet, but the soil will undoubtedly need renewing completely to a depth of 15cm (6in) every few years if problems with disease are to be avoided. Small washed pebbles laid to a depth of 10-15cm (4-6in) are a good alternative. Seeds will still germinate and the birds derive benefit from searching amongst the pebbles. Mice will not take up residence if a good depth of loose pebbles is maintained. Pebbles can easily be riddled to remove waste, washed and disinfected.

Forest bark chippings on an earth floor can look very attractive and again discourage mice if a good covering is maintained. The bark should be about 8-10cm (3-4in) deep and will need to be raked over now and again to freshen it up. It will also need to be removed and replenished from time to time. The spent bark can be composted and used in the garden.

Concrete is sterile and stark and can be cold and damp during inclement weather, but the dampness can be almost eliminated by laying plastic sheeting down before concreting. A layer of sand on top of the finished floor will take away the starkness. It has the advantage of being easy to clean and disinfect and is rodent-proof.

Solid wood floors are also worth considering, having similar benefits to concrete, but being much warmer. However, this type of floor will need to be raised some 30cm (12in) above the ground, allowing a good air flow beneath it to prevent rotting and stopping rodents from gaining access. The whole structure can be set on stilts such as concrete pillars or blocks and bricks with plenty of ventilation holes.

We now come to furnishing the aviary. Most hardbills (and the greenfinch is no exception) quickly defoliate living plants and shrubs. Most will not survive such treatment for long, although vegetation such as elderberry, blackberry and stinging nettles sometimes survive if the aviary is not over-populated. The aviary should be furnished with natural branches such as willow, ash, elder, hazel, apple or pear. These should be located sparsely and high up, providing safe perching and roosting places but still leaving plenty of space for flying exercise.

Since growing shrubs are not usually practical when you are keeping hardbills, substitutes must be provided. There are various ways of doing this using evergreen branches from the conifer tree family. Where single pairs are housed a couple of isolated nesting sites will be found adequate. These are made by wiring a few short branches or twigs of the chosen evergreen around a wickerwork basket or some other similar receptacle (fig 5). For most birds these should be fixed fairly high, close to the roof. Short lengths of gutter down pipe (approximately 15cm (6in) of 6.5cm (2.5in) diameter) screwed to the framework in suitable places as nesting sites can easily be fixed and replaced as required. Where several pairs are housed together at least two such sites must be provided for each pair. They can also be made a little more substantial to give each pair more privacy. This will prove helpful in avoiding the odd skirmish of pairs guarding territory.

For this reason many breeders may find the hedge system suits them better. Strange to say, a continuous hedge all down one side or the back seems to overcome territorial problems, and pairs nest close to each other without any fighting. The artificial hedge is built in the following way. Vertical spacers about 5cm (2in) thick are fastened to the side of the aviary. Then laths are nailed horizontally about 25cm (10in) apart, starting from the top. It is not necessary to go below about 75cm (30in) from the floor. If possible, choose the west or south-west side. If the outside of this part of the aviary is of wood, or some other solid material, so much the better. If not, cover it with hessian or roofing felt to provide protection and privacy. Bare, forked branches are now placed in the laths to simulate the inside of a hedge.

After this, conifer branches or other evergreens such as heather and gorse are threaded into the laths producing a finish rather like an uncut hedge. It is important that this should not be too thick and that there are holes in the foliage through which the birds can obtain access to the inside of the hedge where they will build their nests. Do not forget to put a covering 30-46cm (12-18in) wide on the outside of the aviary over the top of the hedge to provide shade from the sun and shelter from the rain.

If birds are to be kept in a very open-type aviary all the year round, it is best to attach some sort of shelter shed to it so that the feeding takes place inside, and it may be necessary on occasions to confine the birds inside as well. The shelter shed can be as large or small as you desire, or it can be the main bird room with the aviary built on the side. A container full of grit and a bath of fresh water are other essentials to the aviary.

If the birds are being bred in cages in a shed it is very helpful to have a small flight built on to the end of the shed. The birds are fed inside the shed with a pop-hole to give access to the flight. Young birds, when fully weaned, can be transferred to this flight, leaving the parents free to get on with the next nest. Most birds moult out better in a flight where they have access to fresh air with plenty of exercise and bathing facilities.

It is recommended that all birds be ringed, and it is worth bearing this point in mind when deciding on the feeding stations. For some pairs it is a great help if the feeding stations can be somewhat obscured from the nesting sites.

As previously mentioned, aviaries can be as large or small, as ornamental or as heavily-built, as the owner desires, but all will follow the basic pattern of design described and illustrated in the sketches. Refinements can be added according to individual taste.

One point that should be stressed is that it is better not to have the doors too large unless a safety porch is included. If doors are 90cm-120cm (3-4ft) high and approximately 60cm (2ft) wide an area of 60-90cm (2-3ft) will be left above the door on the usual 2m (6ft) aviary. Birds flying towards the door will go to this space above it as you approach and enter, reducing the possibility of escape. The door should be set well clear of the ground so that it opens and closes freely. Doors can open inwards or outwards to suit the needs of the keeper.

Rambler roses, honeysuckle, clematis, hop and other climbing plants can be grown up the outside of the aviary. They look very attractive and help to attract greenfly and other insects from which the birds will benefit. However, the growth must not be allowed to interfere with the general maintenance of the aviary. If the growth should penetrate the wire netting for a prolonged period it can create holes that are large enough to allow birds to escape. This can easily happen before the damage is noticed by the keeper.

Charlock

Evolution

To find out more about our birds and how they live in the wild we must first study how they have evolved. To describe how birds evolved from lizards and acquired the power of flight would take a book on its own, so this chapter is confined to the evolution of the species we know today as the greenfinch.

Evolution has been going on for millions of years and is still continuing today, although we do not notice it. The world is changing all the time, and any species of plant, animal or bird that cannot adapt to these changes dies out and becomes extinct. Evolution either produces a new species or enables an existing one to exploit a new source of food or a new habitat in which to live and breed. However, nature is not quite as simple as that, and there are many complications that we do not yet understand. For example, most species have natural enemies that prey on them. They therefore have to have the ability to avoid them by natural camouflage, running fast, flying, or a combination of abilities. This enables sufficient members of the species to survive and produce further generations.

In all species an individual obtains half its genes from its father and half from its mother, but which genes it receives from which parent is a matter of chance; there are more combinations than on the football pools. It follows that each member of a family is different from its brothers and sisters. Differences are turning up all the time and, if one individual is better able to take advantage of a particular food supply and avoid its natural enemies, it will survive to pass on its genes to the next generation. Nature has no use for those that cannot meet this criterion; they simply become a meal for something else and do not get the chance to breed.

If members of a species are confined to an enclosed geographical location, such as a small island, and a considerable amount of in-breeding takes place among them, the group will develop variations from the main species population, becoming a sub-species. Stock breeders have known this for a very long time and have used it to develop different breeds. For example, the shire horse and the race horse both evolved from the original wild horse. Aviculturists use it to develop the exhibition points that they require, but frequently run into trouble by ignoring nature's basic law: only the fittest and strongest survive to breed.

According to geologists, South Africa and South America

were once joined together, forming one land mass. We also know that there have been a number of ice ages, during which most of Europe and North America were covered in snow and ice. Unable to withstand these conditions, the bird populations would have moved southwards into the African/South American land mass, joining those already residing there. This would explain why many of the birds in the Americas are strikingly similar to European species, varying only in some of their colours. Of course, there are some species in America that do not exist in Europe, and vice versa.

There are several species of siskin in South America, all confined to small areas, with geographical variations of plumage. The North American pine siskin (Carduelis pinus) is similar in many ways to our European siskin (Carduelis spinus). Our summer migrants (like the swallow) all winter in Africa, and the corresponding North American migrants winter in South America. We have been unable to trace any bird in America that is similar to the greenfinch, which suggests that it has evolved much more recently. It would appear that this has only happened since the last ice age, about 15,000 years ago. We can trace the greenfinch back to the serin (Serinus serinus). In comparatively recent times the serin was confined to North Africa and the Mediterranean coast of Europe. It is also found in the Canary Isles where it has developed into a sub-species (Serinus canaria). Approximately 400 years ago this serin was brought to England. Through selective breeding it has evolved into our modern canary. The red canary has been developed by pairing the red hooded siskin (Spinus cucullatus) from South America to the canary,

Lutino greenfinch mule

from which some fertile hybrids were obtained. Fertile hybrids are considered to be proof of a close relationship. The existence of siskins in South America suggests that its ancestors were in South Africa before South America broke away, and it would seem that the siskin and the serin had a common ancestor.

Greenfinch x goldfinch hybrid cock

In this century the serin has extended its range northwards through Europe but, for a long time previously, it was confined to an area south of the Alps and the Pyrenees. As the ice gradually receded at the end of the last ice age the land opened up: first as tundra, but then birch trees developed, then pines, and finally deciduous trees. This enabled plants, animals and birds to move in. Many could only move in during summer to take advantage of the rich feeding for rearing their young, and were forced to return home to Africa for the winter. This process continues to this day with the migratory species. As trees gradually grew higher up the mountains so birds and animals were able to live at higher altitudes. Thus the serin evolved as a mountain bird on the Alps and the Pyrenees, and was called the citril finch *(Serinus citrinella)*. It is still recorded as a serin and, to this day, is confined to these mountains and other mountainous areas to the south. In illustrations the citril finch looks very much like the greenfinch, but is slightly smaller. The greenfinch, though a lowland bird, clearly evolved from the citril finch.

It is interesting to record that there are two other species of greenfinch besides the European. One is the Himalayan greenfinch *(Carduelis spinodes)*, another mountain bird, which has the head and beak of our greenfinch but the body and markings of a siskin *(Carduelis spinus)*. The other is the Chinese greenfinch *(Carduelis sinica)*, sometimes called the oriental greenfinch, which of course lives in China. This bird has the head and beak of our European greenfinch but the body and markings of a goldfinch *(Carduelis carduelis)*. The Himalayan and Chinese greenfinches both produce fertile hybrids when paired to our European greenfinches, proving that they are closely related.

There have been several authenticated cases of siskin mules being fertile when paired back to canaries, though as far as we know it has not been tried the other way round. Mules and hybrids had always been considered sterile. It has been realised only recently that imprinting plays a large part in birds' behaviour and it is possible that hybrids are reluctant to mate with a species other than that which reared them. Experience with the red hooded siskin suggests that only the cocks (and perhaps only some of them) will be fertile in the first generation, though they may have to be two or three years old before they can produce. It is probable that the hens will not be fertile until at least the second, and perhaps even the third or fourth, generation.

It can be seen that canaries, greenfinches, siskins and goldfinches are very closely related, and there could be many possibilities for creating new breeds through hybridisation.

Normal greenfinch cock with agate hen (Left: hen, Right: cock)

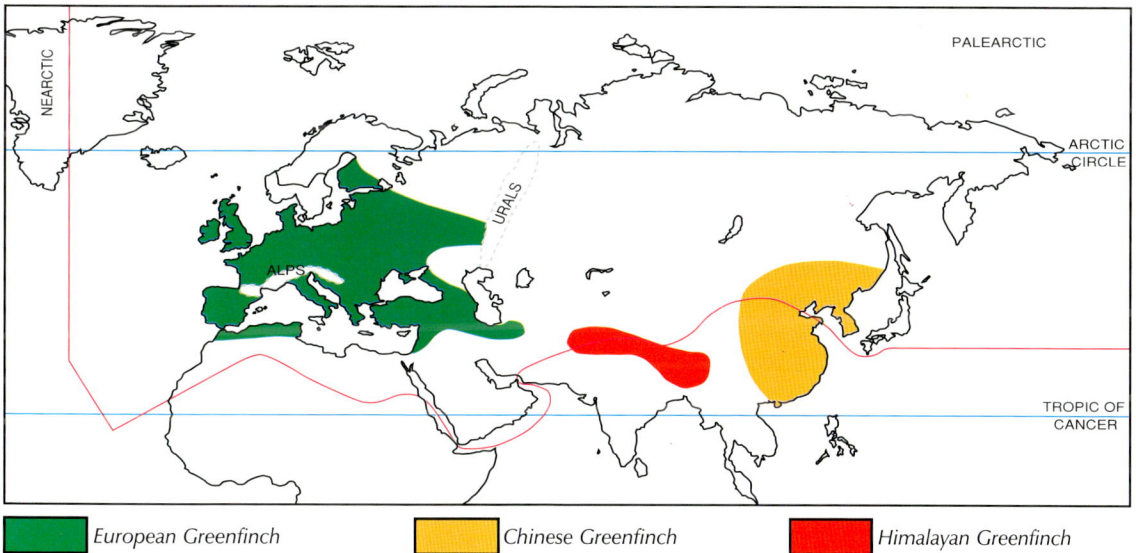

European Greenfinch   Chinese Greenfinch   Himalayan Greenfinch

World-wide distribution of greenfinches

Lifestyle in the Wild

Order: Passeriformes
Family: Fringillidae (Finches)
Sub-Family: Carduelinae
Genus: Carduelis chloris
Common Name: Greenfinch

Description

Length: 14-15cm (5·5-6in)
Weight: Approximately 26g (1oz)
Wingspan: 17.8cm (7in)
Length of Tarsus (leg): 1.8cm (0.7in)

Cock

Olive-green plumage with brighter yellow-green rump and bright yellow patches on the primaries and at the sides of the tail. Jonque (yellow) and mealy (buff) forms are easily distinguishable in this species. The jonque is slightly smaller and much yellower with yellow on the breast. The mealy form is larger and not quite as colourful.

Hen

A much browner bird, more like a sparrow, but with yellow on the outer sides of the primaries, though not to the same extent as the cocks. An easy bird to sex.

Juveniles

Birds which have not yet attained their adult plumage are a similar colour to the hen, but are mottled and streaked until the completion of their first moult at approximately 12 weeks.

Bill

The greenfinch has a stout beak, large skull and powerful jaw muscles, enabling the bird to crush hard seeds. The lower mandible has a chisel-like edge that fits into grooves in each side of the top mandible when the beak is closed. By using its tongue, the bird fits the seed into the groove and splits the seed with the lower mandible. Seeds are placed so that the lower mandible presses directly onto the weakest point.

Legs and Feet

Some finches, because of the length and position of their legs on their bodies, can feed by clinging and hanging upside down on the food plant. The greenfinch cannot to do this, and feeds either on the ground or by standing on the food plant and using its own weight to bend the plant down. This helps to reduce competition between the different species.

Crop

The greenfinch, like many finch-like birds, has a distensible gullet, which it fills with food before passing the food into the stomach for digestion. It can then regurgitate this food and feed it to the young.

Distribution

This bird is common over the whole of the British Isles and Europe. Its range extends northwards as far as the southern parts of Scandinavia and across Russia, eastwards to the Urals and northern Iran, and southwards to north-west Africa and Israel. A small population in the highlands of Russian Turkestan is isolated by a belt of steppe and desert in which the species cannot survive. It is noticeable that the birds in the southerly areas are smaller but more highly coloured; the further north they live, the larger and less coloured they become. There is a considerable difference in both size and colour between those from the furthest south and those from the furthest north. See maps on pages 15 and 18.

Habitat

Originally a woodland bird, the greenfinch is now a bird of forest edge scrub, young conifer plantations, farmlands, orchards, villages, cemeteries, parks, gardens and industrial wasteland. It inhabits almost every part of the countryside that is abundantly supplied with trees, hedges, bushes and evergreens. A sociable bird, it often nests in loose colonies. It is a frequent visitor to bird tables where it is particularly attracted to peanuts.

Migration

The greenfinch is generally considered a resident and sedentary species, and many never go more than 10 miles or so from where it was born. However, in winter there is a general south-westerly movement, particularly from the most northerly part of its range. In autumn Scandinavian birds often arrive along the east coast of England. Being ground feeders, many birds have to move south in severe weather, particularly heavy snow, and birds ringed in England have been found quite long distances away in the south of France.

Flight

This is similar for most finches, slightly undulating, a few rapid wing beats alternating with momentary closure and brief glide, often accompanied by a rapid twitter.

Lifespan

The greenfinch is heavily predated by cats, hawks, owls, magpies, rats, and weasels, and has to be a prolific breeder to survive. At least 75% of the young which fledge die before Christmas. There are other reasons for this besides predation. Severe weather in the winter, when many starve to death, takes a further toll. Very few of those that live to breed see a second breeding season. The average life of those that survive their first winter is 18 months.

Spear thistle

Main foods

Greenfinches feed mainly on seeds produced between May and September, after which remaining stocks are steadily depleted. In summer half-ripe seeds are used as each species becomes available. Food is scarcest in spring and hard weather, because of snow and frost. Like all finches, greenfinches concentrate generally on the largest seeds they can crack, but take advantage of the availability of other seeds as well. They also take a considerable amount of greenfood from plants. Starting in the spring, their main foods are dandelion, chickweed, groundsel, elm, dogs' mercury, charlock and other brassicas, goatsbeard, cultivated cereals, persicaria, burdock, bramble, thistles, yew, hornbeam and rose. Apart from plants, they eat some beetles, caterpillars, aphids and spiders.

Flocking

Greenfinches feed in flocks of mixed species all the year round, including the entire breeding season. In autumn and winter flocks leave the roosts at daybreak in small parties, joining together to form the largest parties in the best feeding areas early in the day when the birds are hungry. During the middle of the day, small parties move away to rest, drink and bathe. There is also movement between the flocks; in fact birds continually move around, both feeding and roosting. Flocks reassemble in the afternoon to feed again. It is important that each bird finds sufficient food to last it through the long night. If it does not it will either die during the night or be so weakened by morning that it provides an easy meal for a predator, especially in severe weather with short days and long nights. Flying birds seeing a group feeding will immediately join them, and the flocks soon build up. This gregariousness helps each individual to find food and gives increased protection from predators. Finches have special alarm calls and, if danger threatens the flock, they take off all together and make for the nearest cover, only to return to feed a few minutes later. In the evening, flocks break up into small parties and fly to the roost in thick scrub, clumps of evergreen, rhododendrons, gorse and conifers. Although the same roosts are used each night, individual birds do not always go to the same one, and the number in each varies considerably from night to night. In early summer the flocks break up into small groups, but return to the flock each day to feed.

Distribution in the British Isles

Courtship and Territory

As the days start to get longer the cocks come into colour and begin to make overtures to the hens in the flock, but may not be accepted. When he eventually finds a hen in a similar stage of breeding condition and who is interested, billing (tapping each other's beaks) commences. Later the cock starts to feed the hen. At this stage the pair will spend more time on its own, but continually returning to the flock. As the daylight improves the birds have more time to feed, and this gradually brings them into breeding condition. In about March, depending on the weather conditions, the pair start to look for suitable nesting sites, which may be some distance from the feeding grounds. The hen eventually selects a place, and the cock sits close by on a prominent twig and sings, proclaiming it his territory. Greenfinches generally do not feed in the vicinity of the nest so there is no need to defend a large territory. Other pairs usually take up positions in quite close proximity, sometimes as little as three metres away.

Nest building does not start straight away. It is dependent on the weather conditions and the availability of suitable food for bringing the birds into full breeding condition and, ultimately, feeding the young. The dandelion is the plant which sets them off, and when the dandelion crop is ripening is when conditions are right for greenfinches to start breeding. As nest building begins the cock starts to display, expanding his tail and offering food to the hen while opening and closing his wings. Another display is a bat-like song flight in which the cock circles round and round with wings flapping slowly. These displays help to stimulate the hen into breeding condition. Singing is normally heard from mid-March to August.

Nesting

Nest building generally begins in early April. The hen builds the nest alone, although she is accompanied by the cock. Their nests are untidy, bulky, but flexible structures, built in hedgerows, evergreens or bushes and usually about 2.5m (11ft) above the ground. They are built with twigs and moss mixed with grass bents and bits of wool, and lined with softer materials such as fine roots, hair and sometimes feathers. Building is carried out from about 9.00 am to 11.00 am and takes about 10 days. However, this can be delayed by a spell of bad weather. Because bushes are in an early state of growth, early nests are more easily discovered and are often predated. If this happens, a new nest in a new place will be started within a few days.

Laying and Incubation

The hen will not necessarily start laying as soon as the nest is completed; when she starts will depend upon the temperature and the availability of sufficient food to form the eggs. For this greenfinches are dependent upon the dandelion, which requires a mean temperature of 13°C (45°F). The dandelion crop is usually available from the first week of April, but this can vary by a couple of weeks either way. Incubation is by the hen alone, beginning after the fourth egg is laid and generally taking approximately 13 days. In cold weather this can be prolonged by several days. During incubation the hen only leaves the nest for a few minutes to defecate, preen, exercise and bathe, usually accompanied by the cock. During the whole of this period the cock feeds the hen by regurgitation. Usually there are three broods or attempted broods but there can be more if some of the broods have been lost for any reason.

Eggs

The eggs are laid daily, usually four in each nest, but sometimes as many as six. The eggs are bluish-white with reddish-brown spotting in varying degrees, mostly on the large end. They are larger than, but in many other respects similar to, the eggs of the siskin and goldfinch, to which the greenfinch is closely related. Eggs weigh approximately a tenth of the weight of the hen; therefore, the larger the hen, the larger the eggs and the resultant chicks. Eggs take several hours to hatch and, when the young chick is dry, the shell is either eaten or carried away.

Young

When the young are small, the cock feeds the hen by regurgitation of the food in his crop and the hen feeds the chicks. The cock flies off to the feeding grounds, which can be up to 2 miles (1.5 kilometres) away. Seed is dehusked, insects are crushed and a few grains of grit and a few sips of water are collected until the cock's crop is full. He then flies back to the nest to feed the hen and the young. This means that they get a feed about every half-hour but, as the chicks also have crops, the parents can fill these at each feed so that the chicks can last out until the next feed arrives. Birds that rear their young entirely on insects do not have a crop and have to feed them every few minutes. Greenfinches feed quite a high proportion of small insects, mainly greenfly, to their newly-hatched chicks but, within a few days, they are weaned onto a diet of half-ripe seed. For the first seven days the hen continues to brood the young and clean their faeces from the nest either by swallowing them or, as the young get older, by carrying them away. At seven days old the young are starting to feather and can generate some heat in the nest themselves. They are now big enough to excrete onto the rim of the nest, so the hen stops cleaning it. She can now spend much more time away from the nest and help the cock to collect food. From now on both the cock and the hen feed the chicks.

Fledging

At about 14 days old the young are fully feathered, although their tails and flight feathers have not yet reached their full length. Full length is achieved in about a further three weeks. The weight of the young is only about two-thirds that of an adult, and full weight is not achieved until the end of the first moult, at about 12 weeks. At between 14 and 16 days old the young leave the nest and perch in the bushes nearby. This may be delayed by several days in bad weather when the parents cannot collect as much food. The cock goes on feeding the young after fledging while the hen begins building the next nest. As the young get stronger and better able to fly they follow the cock to the feeding grounds and eventually join the flock. At about four weeks, they are normally fully weaned and able to look after themselves. If the weather has been continuously bad or food has been very scarce during the rearing period, the smallest and weakest young will have died in the nest. This is nature's way of insuring that at least one or two survive rather than the whole nestful dying of malnutrition.

Cinnamon greenfinch (cock)

Moult

The moult is necessary because, after a year, a bird's feathers become worn and are less effective for flight and insulation. In most birds the moult occurs outside the breeding and migration seasons, but while food is still sufficiently plentiful to support the growth of feathers. However, we do not know exactly what brings on the moult. Reducing daylight length has some effect and perhaps colder nights. Nevertheless, not all birds of any given species finish breeding at the same time, although it is not unknown for a pair to commence a late nest only to abandon it while young are still in the nest and start moulting immediately.

Adult finches replace all their feathers after breeding. Sexual activities cease within a matter of days. The birds become silent and keep mostly in cover. Gonads regress and the sex hormones are replaced by other hormones. The thyroid hormone raises the birds' metabolic rate and controls the growth of new feathers, which are fed from the blood stream, while the skin becomes heavily vascularised instead of being loose and thin.

Feathers are grouped into tracts that run along the length of the body with bare areas of skin in between, as can easily be seen in nestlings. In nestlings, all the feathers grow at the same time until they spread over the whole body. In adults,

Dandelion

new feathers emerge in a regular sequence over a period of several weeks. When one feather is grown, the next is shed, so that the bird is never left naked or unable to fly. (Ducks, geese and swans have a different arrangement.) If feathers are knocked out accidentally outside the moulting season, replacement feathers grow immediately, but not if a feather is just broken. Each growing feather is encased in a sheath or quill containing blood. When the feather is about one third grown it breaks the sheath, which shrinks and finally drops away. Within a few days of the feather completing its growth it hardens, the blood supply stops, and it becomes a dead structure held by the muscles at its base.

In adult finches the first feathers to be shed are the innermost primaries and the outermost secondaries of both wings, the last in each wing being the outermost primaries and the innermost secondaries. The large tail feathers are moulted in pairs, beginning with the central pair. Body feathers are moulted from the centre of each feather tract spreading outwards. In their first moult, juveniles retain their large flight and tail feathers for another year. Apart from this they moult their feathers in the same sequence as adults. Most juveniles moult at about 12 weeks old, but late hatched birds moult before that age, when the adults are moulting.

Feathers consist almost exclusively of keratins, which are proteins containing large amounts of sulphur amino-acids, cystine and methionine. For this reason the birds require a great deal of protein during the moult, which has to come from the food that the birds eat at the time. The true nutritional requirements to provide this are not yet known. The food must be available continuously. Any shortage on even one day is sufficient to cause the formation of a fault bar on the growing feather, which is then liable to break at this point during the year. As well as producing new feathers, the bird loses heat much more easily while moulting, so must eat more. Adults generally take up to 12 weeks to moult completely, usually beginning in August or September.

Feather Type

In most species, including finches, there are two feather types, and a bird has either one or the other.
- A jonque bird has shorter, narrow, silky feathers that are much better coloured and make the bird look brighter but smaller. This is generally known by aviculturists as a yellow, but this name is very misleading, because it does not refer to the colour of the bird.
- A mealy bird has longer, broader, coarser feathers, the tips of which are pale buff or white. The bird has a mealy appearance, but looks larger and duller than the jonque. This is generally known by aviculturists as a buff, but again it is misleading, because it has no direct connection with the colour of the bird, but with its feather type.

In some species it is not always easy to tell the difference, but this does not apply to the greenfinch, on which they are easily distinguishable.

Survival

Only the fittest and strongest shall survive to breed and pass on their genes to the next generation. This is Nature's law throughout the animal kingdom, and every other individual becomes a meal for something else. Nature is very cruel, and greenfinches have a tough time in the wild.

Normal greenfinch pair (Left: cock, Right: hen)

Foods and Accommodation

Greenfinches are ideal subjects for cage and aviary breeding and a good species with which to start breeding British birds. Almost everything that has been said in the previous chapter is applicable to breeding greenfinches in cages and aviaries. Our job is to provide them with proper care and attention in housing, diet and hygiene. Given this, greenfinches kept under domestic conditions can be expected to live an average of six or seven years. Many will live longer and it is not unusual for males to reach twelve years and still remain productive. Females do not usually live quite as long but can be expected to be productive even at six or seven years of age.

ACCOMMODATION

We have already discussed the minimum suitable size of cage in chapter 1 but, as well as providing room for living and breeding, we must consider the need to ring the young if they are to be sold or exhibited. It is best to make the cage so that it can be divided when required. The birds should always have food and water at one end and the nesting site at the other. The parents can then be shut in the feeding end while the young are ringed, and will not be disturbed to the same extent. At the same time, the breeder will have more freedom for the ringing operation.

It goes without saying, the larger the cage the better. Greenfinches confined to the smaller cages normally used for canary breeding often shed their primary wing feathers. Even the slightest of night frights will induce this problem when they are kept in such cages, often at a critical time during the breeding or show season. So the larger the cage provided, the better are the chances of avoiding this problem, to which this species seems rather prevalent.

The problems are not quite the same in aviaries, but access to the nesting site is again important. In a small aviary it is extremely difficult to ring young birds if the parents are dashing about wildly because the breeder is taking up most of the available space. Access from a safety porch is the most convenient, if this can be arranged.

Greenfinches are hardy and can be put into an aviary in the autumn. They will be all the better for wintering outside, provided that they have adequate supplies of food and water. Water is the main problem because it can freeze in hard weather. If the food and water are in a shelter shed to which the birds have access through bob-holes, sufficient heat can generally be provided to maintain the shed just above freezing point, which is all that is necessary. In this case the birds should be kept in the shed for at least a week before being allowed to find their own way through the bob-hole; otherwise they will be very reluctant to enter the shed. Generally, breeders who are away from home all day will find it better to keep the birds inside for winter, transferring them to the aviary as early in the spring as the weather allows. This has the added advantage of giving the flights a rest, when they can be disinfected, reducing the possibility of disease. The ground can be dug over, limed and seeded with grass, allowing the rain, sun and frost to sweeten the earth.

Greenfinches are sociable birds, and several pairs will sometimes breed together in a very large aviary where the continuous artificial hedge described in chapter 1 is used. However, there must never be more cocks than hens, or fighting will ensue. It is usually best to have only one pair in a flight but they can be mixed with other finches provided that they are not overcrowded. Each pair should have a minimum of 2.2 cubic metres (80 cubic feet) of space. This is worked out by multiplying together the length, the width and the height. For example, a flight measuring 2.5m x 1.5m x 2m is equal to 7.5 cubic feet. If this is divided by 3 the answer is 2.5 cubic metres each, so three pairs is the maximum for this flight during the breeding period

FOODS

Very little is known about the correct quantities and various nutrients that a small bird requires to keep it in good condition throughout the different seasons of the year. What information is available has all been obtained by trial and error. We know that birds need carbohydrates, protein, fat, vitamins, minerals and water in differing amounts at different times of the year, but not what makes a balanced diet.

Birds have a built-in mechanism

Himalyan x European greenfinch hybrid F1 cock

for regulating their food intake to their bodily requirements and vary their diets according to the time of the year. It is not entirely practicable to provide each food separately in cages and aviaries so that birds can eat as much or as little of each as they want, but we can supply some of the more important foods separately. Although greenfinches kept in cages are not generally prone to obesity, it is beneficial to restrict them to a diet that is slightly less rich than that given to aviary birds because, being in a more restricted area, they are far less active.

Seeds

A good British finch mixture is recommended as the basic diet. Some excellent mixtures are available on the market, together with some very poor ones. Mixtures are generally made up to feed a variety of species so, when they are fed to a single species or even just a few selected species, there will be considerable wastage. For this reason, the mixture you choose will need to be examined and supplemented as necessary. Different mixtures can also be mixed together to improve the basic mixture. The addition of a good condition mixture and a soak mixture (in the dry state) will also improve the usual finch mixture. Other seeds will have to be added or fed separately to make up a varied and wholesome diet. The following seeds should be provided:

Canary Seed (plain): This is very useful and greenfinches eat it in considerable quantities, especially in the autumn and spring.

Rape Seed or Brassica Seed: These are available in black and red. Given the choice, the greenfinch eats black in preference to red. Considerable quantities will be taken, particularly if it is softened by soaking.

Linseed or Flax: This will be taken in small amounts and is particularly useful during the moult, adding a nice sheen to the plumage.

Niger Seed: This is very nourishing and should be fed in reasonable (not excessive) quantities. It is a good conditioner and helps to prevent egg-binding.

Millet Seeds: The greenfinch is not keen on seeds of the millet family. However, Japanese millet will be taken in reasonable amounts, particularly if it is softened by soaking. Pearl and plate millet will be taken in small amounts and also panicum on the spray.

Hemp Seed: This is a great favourite with greenfinches and, given the chance, they will gorge themselves on it. It is a very important seed, but amounts must be restricted to small quantities daily. Some fanciers prefer to feed this separately rather than in the mixture.

Teasel: Greenfinches are fond of this seed in the heads in the autumn. If the heads are split they extract all the seed in a short time. They also take small amounts during the breeding season, and it is particularly useful when softened by soaking.

Groates - Pinhead Oatmeal: Greenfinches eat quantities of this. It is an excellent food during rearing and also in autumn and winter, but it should be fed sparingly to birds in cages as it can be fattening.

Sunflower Seed: This is a great favourite but, like hemp, must be restricted to a reasonable daily intake. It is best fed separately. Greenfinches accept all varieties of this seed, but the small, striped variety suits them best. When soaked it is an excellent seed for the rearing period.

Safflower Seed: A fairly recent introduction onto the bird seed market, this seed is related to the sunflower, but smaller, with a hard, white outer shell. Once a greenfinch learns how to open them, they are often preferred even to sunflower.

Teasel

Pine Nuts: This is another seed recently introduced onto the market, and a very useful and nourishing food. The small, Chinese variety is about the size of apple pips and greatly enjoyed by greenfinches. They have difficulty in opening the larger Russian variety, but feed on the kernels when the nuts are broken open for them.

Maw Seed (Dutch Blue): This poppy seed is usually included in condition mixtures. This tiny seed appears to have medicinal properties to tone up the system. Birds search for it, consuming considerable amounts. Among other seeds used as conditioners and frequently included in condition seed mixtures for their medicinal properties are gold of pleasure, sesame, dandelion, lettuce, marigold, chicory, celery and carrot. All are useful seeds when fed in small amounts.

Soaked Seed Mixtures: These contain a variety of the above seeds, selected for their ability to soften and germinate quickly when soaked for a short period. They are particularly useful during the breeding and moulting seasons. The mixture should be soaked for 48 hours in clean water, which must be changed two or three times during this period; otherwise the seed will sour and smell. The mixture should be washed in a sieve under a running tap and drained before it is fed to the birds. Soaked seeds are a substitute for the semi-ripe and naturally soft seeds obtained by birds in the wild that at times forms the bulk of their diet.

Egg Foods (Rearing and Condition Foods)

These are available in a wide variety. Greenfinches accept these foods and they should be considered essential during rearing and weaning times. If any birds are reluctant to take them they can soon be encouraged to do so if they are kept with a few birds such as canaries that take them freely. They can also be induced to take reasonable amounts if the egg food is mixed in equal amounts with soaked seeds, and a little maw seed or niger added. These soft foods are high in protein and are used as a substitute for animal protein, which birds in the wild obtain by taking small aphids, flies, and caterpillars.

Mealworms

Most greenfinches will not take these outside the breeding season but soon learn to take them when rearing young. They provide a suitable animal protein. If your greenfinches are reluctant to take them, redpolls and siskins are excellent teachers.

Mealworms are best offered as a titbit in the spring, one or two per bird, with soft food. They should be broken or beheaded to immobilise them. The birds do not usually consume the whole mealworm, but extract the contents, leaving the skin.

When greenfinches hatch young, the supply should be increased to about 20 a day. However, do not provide an unlimited supply because too many mealworms can have a detrimental effect on both young and adults, being very high in protein but lacking in calcium.

Grits

Since birds do not have teeth they eat grit and small stones, which are used in their gizzards to grind up foods. Seed eaters such as greenfinches consume quite large quantities. Good clean grits should always be readily available.

Charcoal (Granulated)

This also is consumed in fair quantities. It acts as an internal cleanser, removing toxins and purifying the system. It can be either mixed with grits or supplied separately.

Cuttlefish Bone (calcium)

All birds require calcium, and cuttlefish is a good way of providing a constant supply. Hens in particular consume large amounts, which they need for the formation of egg shells and for the development of strong bones in their young. A shortage can lead to problems such as soft-shelled eggs and rickets. Although birds store calcium in their bodies, a supply should be available to them at all times.

Water

A permanent supply of fresh water is essential. A shallow vessel containing water not more than 3cm (1.5in) deep, replenished daily, provides for both drinking and bathing. Most birds cannot live more than a few hours without water and, if there is a shortage, they soon dehydrate. The intake of water is increased during egg laying and rearing of young, and any shortage soon causes serious losses. Bathing is essential to enable the birds to keep their feathers in good condition.

Coltsfoot

Greenfood

Some breeders and some scientific authorities claim that greenfoods are of no dietary value, but even those with such opinions have to agree that most birds appear to derive great pleasure from eating them. Even if this is the only benefit, then surely they should be included in the diet. Other fanciers, such as ourselves, believe that greenfoods, whether cultivated or wild plants, should be considered an essential part of the bird's diet throughout the year. They provide vitamins, minerals and trace elements. During the coldest winter months they are not so necessary and can be reduced to very small amounts. In any case, frosted greenfoods should never be fed, as they will purge the birds. During cold periods a small slice of sweet apple, cucumber, celery, swede or carrot can be offered. Gradually, amounts of greenfood can be increased during spring into the breeding and moulting periods, decreasing after the moult has finished.

The following cultivated plants will be taken freely: all members of the Brassica family such as brussel sprout, cabbage, kale, rape. Spinach, lettuce, land-cress, and water-cress will also be acceptable.

If you can gather wild plants from clean, non-polluted areas then there are many plants of which the greenfinch is particularly fond, either in the 'green' or 'semi-ripe' stage:

Chickweed: This is possibly the most valued of all weeds and is available all the year round. All parts of the plant will be eaten, the semi-ripe seeds being taken in large quantities during the rearing periods.

Groundsel: Another plant available during most of the year. The seeding heads can be given in quantity, but the leaves have a laxative effect and should be fed more sparingly, particularly if the birds have previously been starved of greenfoods for some time.

Coltsfoot: The harbinger of spring. Its seeding heads are valued as a conditioner just prior to the breeding season.

Plantain

Dandelion: Another valuable spring conditioner. All parts of the plant will be taken: fresh young leaves and roots in early spring, followed by the semi-ripe seeding heads (particularly useful during rearing the first round of chicks), and the ripened seed heads can be gathered and the seed stored for autumn and winter use.

Sowthistle and Milkthistle: These plants are a great favourite during the breeding season; seeding heads, young leaves, and stems will all be eaten. These plants are also hosts to greenfly and other aphids, which will be much appreciated as an addition to the diet.

Charlock: This and other members of the mustard plant family are all favoured by greenfinches and are extremely useful during the rearing and moulting periods.

Others: Among many other wild-growing plants useful in a greenfinch's diet are shepherds purse, wall lettuce, persicaria, docks, plantain, wild-marigold, knotgrass, rye-grass, common annual grass, meadowsweet and mugwort. The last named plant, mugwort *(Artemisia vulgaris)*, is often neglected by fanciers, and yet it is a most useful plant during the moulting period. The birds spend hours taking the tiny seeds and whittling away at leaves and stems. If tied in bundles it does not shed its seeds easily and can be used during the winter months to keep the birds busy.

Normal greenfinch cock with Isabel hen (Right: hen, Left: cock)

Curled dock

Supplements

A bird's exact requirements are unknown, but few additives are needed if a full and varied diet is provided throughout the year. Some breeders add supplements to the main foods to overcome possible shortages, particularly in vitamins and minerals. Care must be taken not to exceed the recommended quantities.

ABIDEC*: This is a very useful vitamin supplement and is best added to the drinking water. There are many other useful multi-vitamin type supplements on the market, any one of which should meet your birds' needs.

Cod Liver Oil: This is a rich source of vitamin D and can be given throughout the breeding season and during the moult. One teaspoonful is mixed thoroughly with one pound of seed, which is allowed to stand for 24 hours before being fed to the birds.

PYM*: Yeast can be mixed with seed in almost any quantities, as can mineral mixtures, especially those containing iodine. These are a good help in maintaining healthy condition.

Tonics: These can be useful, especially the ones containing iron.

Probiotics: These encourage and build up the 'friendly' bacteria whose function is to keep all the 'unfriendly' bacteria in the gut in check. Probiotics can be given daily throughout the year in the drinking water. (Dosage is as instructed by the product manufacturer.)

* Registered Trade Mark

Watercress

Ragwort

Breeding

You cannot go far wrong by following the birds' lifestyle in the wild, described in chapter 3, but the information given here appertains particularly to birds being kept in cages and aviaries.

Pairing

The usual advice is to pair up the birds when they come into breeding condition. The cocks will be singing and frequently uttering the distinctive drawn-out 'tzee-ee' call. The hen will be bright-eyed, active and generally in good condition. However, it must be remembered that greenfinches in the wild pair up while in the flocks during the winter. For this reason, cocks and hens should be kept separated during the winter, or they form attachments that can lead to difficulties when we try to pair them as we want. It is best to put selected pairs together in the preceding months and keep them together until it is time to put them out into the breeding pen or flight. The pair then gradually come into breeding condition together, the hen exciting the cock and the cock's singing helping to bring the hen forward. Kept like this the birds remain paired and you will avoid any fighting. This method is particularly recommended if a trio (one cock to two hens - *never* the other way round) is to be used.

Nesting

Suitable nesting sites have already been discussed in chapter 1. Greenfinches are early nesters and, in the wild, start in April when the new crop of wild seeds becomes available, particularly dandelion and chickweed. Quantities of both should be provided. For nest building, provide some small birch twigs for the foundation and moss, small roots, coconut fibre, dried grass and cow or dog hair for the lining. If you can obtain it you should also provide sizal string that has been teased out and cut into 5cm (2in) lengths. This is very popular with the birds. Most finches like cotton wool, but it must be used carefully; otherwise it may become tangled in their feet. Buy cotton wool in small rolls, which should not be unrolled, but tied tightly with string or wire and fastened onto the branches in the open where the rain can get at it. The birds will then pull off small beakfuls as they require it and no harm will come to them. If obtainable, white cotton Kapok used for stuffing soft toys and furnishings is better than cotton wool. However, fibres containing nylon must be avoided at all costs, because even the tiniest strand can become entangled on the birds' feet and, if not noticed in time, could soon cause the loss of a toe or even a foot. Dry moss is like a sponge and will keep returning to its original shape so that the birds are unable to mould it into the shape that they require. For this reason, it should be supplied damp or wet, so that the birds can pull it about until they have the right amount of dampness. The hen can then weave and mould the materials and line the nest with dry fibre to fit her body, so that she can brood the eggs properly. A well-constructed nest is strong, secure and flexible so that it will expand as the young grow.

Greenfinches have two or three nests each season.

Brooding

After laying the third or fourth egg, the hen will go broody and start sitting. She may lose the inner feathers on her breast, leaving bare skin known as the 'brood patch'. This allows her to have bodily contact with the eggs, so warming them. When she is not sitting the flank feathers cover the brood patch so that it is not seen.

The eggs hatch in approximately 13 days, although in very cold weather they may take a day or two longer. The hen goes on brooding the young for 7-10 days, until they are feathering and large enough to generate their own heat. Some pairs, although quite tame, resent interference with their nest, so unnecessary investigation should be avoided. Watch out for egg shells on the flight floor; this is a sign that the young have hatched. However, most greenfinches soon learn to tolerate a discreet inspection of the nest once a day or every second or third day. This allows you to keep proper records and there will be fewer problems when you have to visit the nest to ring the young birds. Really it is a matter of getting to know your birds and, perhaps more importantly, your birds getting to know you.

Pastel greenfinch (cock)

Rearing

During courting, and while the hen is sitting, the cock feeds her by regurgitation and she leaves the nest only occasionally, for a few minutes, to defecate and have a quick feed and drink. When the young hatch he continues to feed her and she feeds the young while they are small. After a few days she will allow the cock to feed the young sometimes and, after about seven days, both cock and hen spend their whole time collecting food and bringing it to their young. Some young cocks may be troublesome when first allowed to the nest to feed the youngsters. If this proves to be the case they are best removed, leaving the hen to rear by herself.

If possible, get the greenfinches used to the rearing foods, as previously described, before the breeding season. Once the young hatch, this should be fed at least twice daily, as they require large quantities of protein. Young birds grow at a tremendous rate. In approximately two weeks from being hatched, blind, helpless and naked, they become full-sized birds with full sets of feathers. In the wild the protein is provided in the form of small flies, gnats and especially greenfly.

In an aviary, if space allows, a patch of nettles, some rotting fruit (particularly bananas) and a pile of horse or cow manure attract small insects and keep the parents occupied in collecting them. Half-ripe seeds such as dandelion, chickweed and groundsel are also needed. Groundsel can soon dry out, but lasts better if placed in jars of water. If the jars are sunk into the aviary floor they will not tip over. However, make sure that no bird, particularly youngsters, can fall in and drown. Soaked seed is also necessary to supplement the half-ripe seeds. Only as much as the birds will eat should be given each day because soaked seeds soon dry out and cease to attract them. You can encourage the birds to take more rearing food by mixing it with equal quantities of soaked seeds.

The young birds fledge at 14-19 days, depending on the weather and how well the parents have fed them, and are self-supporting about two weeks after that. The cock may go on giving them some

Siskin x greenfinch hybrid (cock)

food a little longer than this. When you are breeding them in cages the young should be removed as soon as they are self-supporting, but young can be left in the aviary as long as it does not become over-crowded. If a spare aviary is available, cage- and aviary-bred young can both benefit from being transferred to this while they mature. This is when the young birds must have soaked seeds and all the seeding weeds that you can collect. Apart from the seeds on the weeds they also find many small insects on them. Greenfood is also needed, and one way of providing it is by growing grasses. If seed trays of growing grass are supplied the birds will spend a great deal of time pecking in the soil and picking up odd things that we cannot see. It is not known whether these are minerals or small insects, but there is no doubt that they are important to them.

Young greenfinches are particularly prone to 'going light'; that is, they gradually waste away. This happens between fledging and completing their first moult. Once through the moult they are usually safe. Nobody actually knows why they are more prone to this than other species. In the wild they would not be eating hard seeds until well into the winter when they would be through the moult. Experience has shown that young birds that are given only hard seeds nearly always go light. The first signs of going light are the bird fluffing up its feathers and constantly searching for food, always seeming hungry but actually eating very little. Within a few days the bird has

Groundsel

wasted away and died. Four to twelve weeks old is the most vulnerable time. Some youngsters are affected even before leaving the nest.

Many breeders today use Sulphamezathine, or some other sulphur-based drug containing oxytetracycline obtainable on a veterinary surgeon's prescription, as a preventative. The dosage instructions are supplied with the product. It is administered for three to five days, then suspended for a similar period, followed by a further dosage. This procedure has to be repeated at regular intervals during the breeding season and through the moult. After treatment, and during intervals between treatment, a vitamin supplement should be given. This system has been found to be very successful, but the trouble with antibiotics is that they can kill the 'good bugs' as well as the 'bad bugs', possibly leaving the birds susceptible to other diseases. Recently probiotics, said to increase the 'good bugs', which will then fight off the 'bad bugs', have come onto the market. This sounds a better proposition but, at the time of writing, there has not been sufficient time to try it out properly and assess its potential.

It should be recorded that many breeders do not use drugs and have largely overcome the problem of going light by careful feeding, as described above, and good hygiene, combined with retaining only the strongest of the stock for future breeding. However, trials carried out have given good results so far.

Moult

The moult generally begins in August or September, at the end of the breeding season. Nobody knows what actually triggers it off, and not all the birds in a collection start moulting at the same time. Birds with a late nest usually finish rearing their young, but sometimes the moult seems to overtake them and they abandon the nest. Some birds may start to moult as early as August, others much later. The moult puts a heavy strain on their constitution and it is a time when they need the best feeding you can provide. At this time, nature produces an abundance of seeding weeds, a good supply of which will help the birds through the moult and enhance colour and feather quality.

Chapter 6

Ringing Birds

While it is permissible to keep greenfinches that are not ringed, it is illegal to buy, sell or exhibit a greenfinch that is not ringed with an approved closed ring of the correct size. At present there are two approved legal rings:

- The British Bird Council ring, which is exclusive to the British bird fancy.
- The IOA ring, which is used for different types of birds and by exhibitors who may wish to send their birds to shows abroad. At present, quarantine and import/export regulations make exhibiting abroad very difficult. However, closer ties with Europe could see some beneficial changes in the regulations in the near future.

The British Bird Council Ring is brown, and the letters 'BC' are stamped across it, followed by a size letter and serial number. Since 1991 rings also carry a year date. A great deal of work has been done over the years to find the best size for each species, and for greenfinches it is Size E. This ring has to be put on the young bird while it is still in the nest and is acceptable to the authorities as proof that the bird is aviary-bred.

One problem with the closed ring is that some birds resent either the interference in the nest or the foreign object on the chicks. For this reason, the parent birds must be accustomed to the owner and, if possible, reasonably tame before the breeding season. Ringing of the chicks should take place between five and seven days, depending on the rate of growth of the young and the breeder's experience. An inexperienced breeder will probably have to ring earlier than one who is more used to it. The later the ringing takes place, the less are the chances of rejection. This is because the hen no longer needs to remove the faecal sacs from the nest once the chicks start to void their faeces over the side of the nest, so she is no longer so meticulous in cleaning the nest out.

Rings that are fitted too early come off in the nest and are lost. If the ring can be removed easily after fitting it is best to leave it for a further day or two. This can arise particularly when the growth of chicks is staggered because they have hatched on different days. There are usually fewer problems with owner-bred hens than with bought-in stock. With newly-purchased hens it is best to be cautious and ring only the largest chick in the nest to begin with. If this is not mutilated or rejected, it is usually safe to ring the rest of the chicks.

However, if all is not well, do not attempt to ring the remaining chicks under this hen. These chicks will either have to be left unringed or fostered out to a more reliable hen. Many breeders keep a few pairs of canaries to act as foster parents in such cases.

The time of day chosen to ring chicks will depend on the breeder's own circumstances. Some breeders like to ring towards dusk in the belief that the hen will settle down on the ringed chicks. However, if she is going to reject them, she will undoubtedly do so when cleaning the nest the following morning. For this reason, some breeders like to ring in the early morning so that a watch can be kept on the hen. If she rejects, the chicks can be picked up before they expire and either put back with their rings removed or fostered out. If a hen accepts her chicks being ringed, it really makes little difference what time of day you ring them. However, it is sensible to provide some rearing food or favourite seeding weeds to keep the hen busy while you ring the chicks.

For the inexperienced breeder, who will undoubtedly take some time to complete the ringing operation, it is best to leave one chick in the nest. The remainder can be removed and placed in a lined canary nest pan or something similar. Leaving one chick in the nest prevents the hen from being concerned if she returns before ringing is completed. Do not expect to ring chicks easily the first time you try. It takes practice and experience to become proficient. Many breeders find it necessary to ring the birds before they are seven days old, but they should be aware of the problems. It is well worth practising on canaries and budgerigars, which are much more tolerant of interference.

The recommended method for ringing is as follows (see illustrations below):

- As you look at the rings you will see that they are tapered slightly (caused by stamping the number on them). Always place the big end on first.
- It is essential to get the three long toes straight and parallel to each other. If the toes are crossed the ring will not go on. Sometimes it takes several goes to get the ring in this position (fig 1) because the young bird continually tries to clench its toes.
- Having got that far a gentle pressure and slight twisting motion will take the ring up over the ball of the foot (figs 2 and 3).
- The ring is then slid up the shank of the leg until the hind claw is released (figs 4 and 5).

Do not try to rush the job; it requires care and patience. Rings can be obtained by post from The British Bird Council.

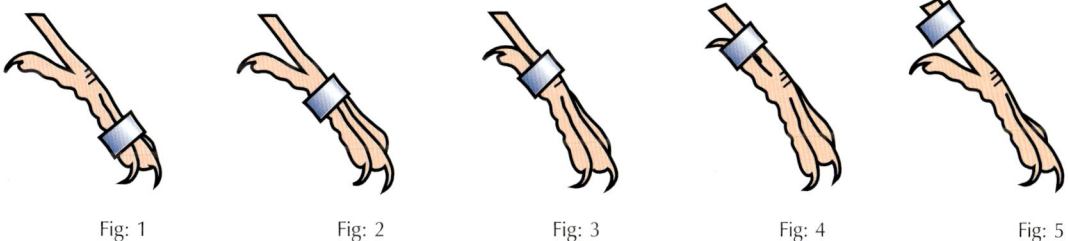

| Fig: 1 | Fig: 2 | Fig: 3 | Fig: 4 | Fig: 5 |

Ringing young birds

Exhibition

The most important rule if you are to be successful on the show bench is to ensure that your birds have access to water for regular bathing. Some birds are reluctant to bathe, but usually follow suit when they see or hear other birds doing so. If they will not, or do not have access to bathing facilities, they should be sprayed regularly. Many successful exhibitors spray their birds if necessary, but prefer a bird to bathe naturally; the majority will, if given the opportunity. When a bird bathes, it relaxes, allowing the water to penetrate the feather; when sprayed, it behaves as if it is trying to avoid the water, 'tightening up'. Birds soon accept spraying, however, and many look forward to and enjoy it. Without any doubt, rain water is best for their plumage. This is what wild birds use and they always carry a 'sheen' or gloss on the feather, obtained by bathing frequently.

A bird should get used to its show cage before it is exhibited. Some birds take to a show cage 'like a duck to water' as the saying goes, but others do not like to be confined. Such birds should be run into show cages for very short periods initially; eventually they will get accustomed to them. Occasionally one does meet a problem bird, but it is surprising how it will accept a show cage in time. Very often a bird, when shown at a small show for a few hours, gains confidence. Once acquired, it is never lost.

Some birds - just a few - have a nasty habit of facing the back of the cage. Such birds seldom overcome the habit. The ideal exhibition bird always faces the front of the cage. Any bird that proves difficult will need patience. Never push a bird so hard that you destroy its confidence. A few will never be steady enough for showing and these are best kept purely for breeding purposes.

When dealing with current-year birds, you should limit their training to short periods at first, returning them immediately after each session to their normal living quarters. Young birds are much more vulnerable to stress than adults, and losses will be experienced if they are put under too much stress too early in their lives. Never be in too much of a hurry to steady down that promising youngster. Patience is the key if you want to avoid disappointments.

The staging or presentation of British seedeaters, mules and hybrids is very important if the exhibitor is to be

Isabel greenfinch x crossbill hybrid (hen)

successful. There is a slight difference in the sizes of show cages advocated by the Scottish British Bird and Mule Club, but we are all agreed that green is the acceptable colour for interiors and black for exteriors. It is very important that exhibits are staged in the sizes advocated for the particular species. It is always permissible to use a larger cage but never a smaller one. Please remember that the sizes recommended and adopted are the minimum sizes and, in the main, the most suitable.

It is most important that show cages are made by skilled cage makers who specialise in this particular job. It is also very important that internal and external decoration of the show cage is of the highest standard.

Sometimes we see show cages that are poorly constructed and decorated. A good bird deserves a good cage; it certainly enhances a bird's chances on the show bench.

To maintain show cages in good condition it is important that you always clean them after a show; wash them thoroughly, particularly the perches, and place them in your carrying case ready for your next show. They also need repainting periodically. If a little polish is put on the cage prior to the show, cleaning with warm water is easy afterwards.

It must be pointed out to those just beginning to exhibit birds that they are only allowed to be kept in show cages for 72 hours and while being transported to and from the shows. Also, it is only permissible to confine a bird in a show cage for training for a maximum of one hour in any 24. At other times, the birds must be kept in their aviaries or in the recommended stock cages.

The full specification of the show cage (size 3) for the greenfinch is:

Length: 30.5cm (12in)
Height: 25.5cm (10in)
Width: 12.75 cm (5in)
Gauge wires: No 14, set at 2cm (0.75in) centres
Drinking hole: 3cm (1.125in) diameter
Bottom rail: 3.75cm (1.5in) high
Top rail: Shaped - 2.5cm (1in) at the outside, sloping to 1.25cm (0.5in) at the centre
Floor coverings: Seed only

The recommended colours are black outside, top, bottom, back and sides, with a bright medium gloss green inside, on the outside of the wires and on both top and bottom rails. All drinkers should be painted green to match or be made of green plastic.

The Scottish Pattern show cage is the same, except that the length is 28cm (11in) instead of 30.5cm.

In an exhibition greenfinch, overall size is important; it should be thick-set, having plenty of width and frontal rise in the skull. It should have a well-rounded head set on a thick, well-defined neck, compatible with body size, and short, compact wings with well-defined yellow bars and well-defined yellow edging to the feathers in the tail. The body should be as clear and bright a green as possible, devoid of smokiness. The bird should be a nice cobby shape, sturdy, and have an upright stance.

Exhibition Standard for Normals

Size: Large as possible. 30 points
Type: Broad, well-rounded head, with good rise and well-cushioned at front, set on full neck and nicely-rounded, really short, thick-set body of strong appearance. Set well across the perch. 30 points.
Colour and Markings: A rich bright green throughout the body. Wings and tail black with slight grey, outer webbing to show bright golden yellow markings. Hens to be of rich brownish and olive hues. Yellow in wings and tail not so intensive or extensive. 20 points
Feather Quality and Condition: 5 points
Steadiness and Presentation: 15 points
Total: 100 points

> **Notes -** Yellows and buffs are evident. Buffs, though being of less intensive colour, shall still be given due consideration. Where yellow and buff exhibits are of equal merit, yellow to take precedence. However, where a buff of good, rich colour is of superior type, buff to take precedence.

> **Faults -** Colour impurities such as smokiness or too much grey suffusion, excessive frosting, too much black suffusion giving a dark appearance, eye defects, deformities, poor presentation, insufficiently trained.

Agate greenfinch (cock)

British Colour Variant Exhibition Standards

The following exhibition standard of points shall apply irrespective of species:

Type: As per normal in all respects. 35 points

Colour and Markings: As per standard for variety. 35 points

Size: As large as possible but only to take precedence when exhibits are considered of equal merit in regard to type and colour. 15 points

Lutino greenfinch (hen)

Condition and Presentation: Clean, steady, of good bloom, well presented. 15 points

Total: 100 points

> **Notes -** Where yellow and buff exhibits are considered of equal merit, yellow to take precedence, however, where a buff of good rich colour is of superior type, buff to take precedence.
>
> **Faults -** Poor type, bad wing carriage, eye defects, deformities, insufficiently trained, poor presentation.

Lutino greenfinch (cock)

Colour Standard

Greenfinch, Cinnamon: A rich golden cinnamon brown, as evenly coloured as possible throughout body, slight green suffusion to be minimised. Wings and tail a somewhat darker shade of brown. Tail and wing primaries to show bright golden yellow. Eyes light brown.

> **Notes -** Yellows and Buffs are evident. Buffs, though being of less intensive colour, showing more frosting, shall still be given due consideration.
>
> **Female -** As above, but of less intensive colour.
>
> **Faults -** Patchy or washed out colour. Excessive frosting.

Greenfinch Lutino: A rich yellow as evenly coloured as possible throughout body. Wings and tail pale yellow. Tail and wing primaries to show bright golden yellow. Eyes clear red.

> **Notes -** Yellows and Buffs are evident. Buffs, though being of less intensive colour, showing more frosting, shall still be given due consideration.
>
> **Female -** As above, but of less intensive colour.
>
> **Faults -** Colour impurities or suffusions, excessive frosting.

Greenfinch Satinette (cinnamon-Ino): A rich yellow with light cinnamon suffusion, as evenly coloured as possible throughout body. Wings and tail pale cinnamon, with darker central webbing giving a laced effect. Tail and wing primaries to show bright golden yellow. Eyes deep red.

> **Notes -** Yellows and buffs are evident, buffs though being of less intensive colour, showing more frosting, shall still be given due consideration.
>
> **Female -** as above, but of less intensive colour.
>
> **Faults -** Patchy or poor cinnamon suffusion, excessive frosting.

Greenfinch Agate (dark-eyed - normal dilute): A rich bright lime green, overlaid with ash grey, showing good ground colour at all colour points. Wings and tail dark grey, almost black, with light grey outer webbing. Tail and wing primaries to show bright golden yellow. Eyes brown.

> **Notes -** Yellows and buffs are evident. Buffs, though being of less intensive colour, showing more frosting, shall still be given due consideration.
>
> **Female -** Dark ash grey above with olive green suffusion, light ash grey, suffused yellow below, showing good ground colour at all colour points, secondaries to show clearly defined dark central webbing.
>
> **Faults -** Colour impurities, excessive frosting or masking of ground colour.

Greenfinch Isabel (cinnamon - normal dilute): A rich bright yellow, overlaid with light cinnamon brown, showing good ground colour at all colour points. Wings and tail a somewhat darker brown with pale outer webbing. Tail and wing primaries to show bright golden yellow. Eyes light brown.

> **Notes -** Yellows and buffs are evident. Buffs, though being of less intensive colour, showing more frosting, shall still be given due consideration.
>
> **Female -** Of rich creamy cinnamon suffusion, showing good ground colour at all colour points. Secondaries to show clearly defined darker central webbing.
>
> **Faults -** Colour impurities excessive frosting or masking of ground colour.

Others: At the time of compiling this book, exhibition standards for pastels, pieds and their composite varieties have not been drawn up, so for the present these variations remain non-standardised.

Mules and Hybrids

Mule is the fancier's term for offspring raised from a canary and a British finch; offspring from two British finches of different species are referred to as hybrids. Both types are really hybrids, and some show schedules refer to mules as canary hybrids. Mules and hybrids are bred for exhibition, song or ornamental purposes and are generally considered to be infertile. However, modern knowledge and the production of the red canary from the red-hooded siskin of South America suggest that some mules may be fertile when paired back to canaries, but perhaps not until they are two or three years old.

Good exhibition mules are produced from Norwich type canaries and sometimes from cross-breeds. The Norwich x Yorkshire cross has been used, and birds of a long-barrel type are preferred by some breeders. Best quality mules are generally obtained from jonque hens, either clear or lightly marked. Good greenfinch mules are not considered easy to produce and better results have been obtained by pairing a canary cock to a greenfinch hen. In this case it is most important to use the best Norwich type cock obtainable.

Both the greenfinch and the canary are early breeders and they should come into breeding condition about the same time. But both birds should be put together in a large cage or small aviary well before breeding condition is reached, by the beginning of January at the latest, to avoid any quarrelling. From then on they should be treated just like the other greenfinches and canaries in your possession. If the first nest should prove infertile, remove the eggs, but leave the birds together and let them try again. When the young leave the nest a clean nest pan should be introduced. About a fortnight later, when the young mules are feeding themselves, they should be removed and placed in a clean, large cage. They should be provided with plenty of egg food and water, together with soaked seed and greenfood.

Many interesting and attractive colour variant mules and hybrids can be produced from the greenfinch when it is crossed with other species, but many colour variant mules produced will be small in size. This is because so many of the mutation colour canaries available are themselves small. Large exhibition mules are bred from large Norwich type canaries, and it is generally only possible to produce large colour variant mules from these by using visual or split-colour variant cock greenfinches, although good-sized cinnamon

mules are produced using cinnamon or split-cinnamon Norwich cocks paired to greenfinch hens. By transferring other canary colour mutations to larger Norwich type stock it is possible to use these to produce good-sized colour variant exhibition mules in a much wider range of colours.

Now that so many colour variants are being bred, it is possible to produce a large number of colour variant hybrids, several of which make attractive exhibition birds. If you seek new challenges, this field certainly has much to offer.

Hybrids are usually bred in small aviaries or larger cages because they generally require more room than muling pairs. Any hybrids produced can be difficult to rear. Some pairs behave perfectly if supplied with all the natural food we can possibly gather while others, for various reasons, do not rear their young. Bullfinch hens are particularly tricky. In this case you could transfer the eggs to a reliable canary hen and leave her to rear those that hatch on the same diet as that on which she would rear her own young, with the addition of seeding weeds and grasses such as chickweed and dandelion. The greenfinch hen usually makes an excellent parent and can be left to hatch and rear her own eggs.

When young hybrids leave the nest they should not be removed from their parents until they are eating well for themselves. When weaned they should be provided with egg food, the usual seed mixture, natural food, and a shallow dish of water so that they can bathe.

You do not have to ring mules and hybrids, although you can if you wish. Whether ringed or not they can legally be bought, sold and exhibited, provided that both parents are listed on Schedule 3 Part 1 of the Wild Life and Countryside Act 1981. (The canary can be one parent provided that the other is on Schedule 3 Part 1.) At the time of writing this act is under review. Hopefully any changes will be beneficial to this side of our hobby.

Exhibition birds should show clearly the characteristics of both

Agate greenfinch (hen)

parents and be of good size in relation to the species from which they are bred. They must have good colour. Mules and hybrids, other than some colour variants, are always colour fed for exhibition. They must be of nice cobby type and excel in quality and condition of feather. Goldfinch, redpoll, siskin, linnet, twite, crossbill and canary cocks have all produced hybrids when paired to greenfinch hens. The reverse matings have also been successful. In addition, the greenfinch cock has produced hybrids when paired to bullfinch, chaffinch and brambling hens.

Mutations & Colour Variants

It is not the intention of this book to delve too deeply into the world of genetics. However, some basic understanding of the genetic inheritance patterns of colour mutations is necessary if we are to control, improve and generally make the best use of these mutations.

There are three basic modes of inheritance: dominant, recessive sex-linked and recessive autosomal. If we were to look deeper within each of these groups we would find deviations such as incomplete dominants and full dominants, multiple alleles and deep recessives. If you wish to delve further into the subject you will find that many books have been published about it.

MUTATION INHERITANCE CHARTS

The following charts are for the guidance of those taking up the breeding of colour variants and can be applied to any species. However, they refer only to pairings involving the use of a single mutated colour form with that of pure normal, not to cross-colour pairing expeditions. The latter involve more than one colour form and are covered elsewhere.

Note

In the charts and pairing expectations used throughout, the cock is always listed first in the pairings and the following symbols are used:

/   denotes 'split', carrier of the mutation.

-     a dash between two varieties refers to a composite variety.

SF   denotes single-factor dominant

DF   denotes double-factor dominant

=   denotes progeny expectations

Recessive, Sex-linked Mutation Chart (referred to as **Sex-linked**)

Normal/Sex-linked	x	Normal	=	Normal Cocks, Normal/Sex-linked Cocks, Normal Hens, Sex-linked Hens
Normal	x	Sex-linked	=	Normal/Sex-linked Cocks, Normal Hens
Normal/sex-linked	x	Sex-linked	=	Normal/Sex-linked Cocks, Sex-linked Cocks, Normal Hens, Sex-linked Hens
Sex-linked	x	Normal	=	Normal/Sex-linked Cocks, Sex-linked Hens
Sex-linked	x	Sex-linked	=	Sex-linked Cocks, Sex-linked Hens

Recessive Autosomal Mutation Chart (referred to as **Recessive**)

Normal/Recessive	x	Normal	=	Normal Cocks, Normal/Recessive Cocks, Normal Hens, Normal/Recessive Hens
(Reverse Pairing gives same expectations)				
Normal/Recessive	x	Normal/Recessive	=	Normal Cocks, Normal/Recessive Cocks, Recessive Cocks, Normal Hens, Normal/Recessive Hens, Recessive Hens
Recessive	x	Normal	=	Normal/Recessive Cocks, Normal/Recessive Hens
(Reverse Pairing gives same expectations)				
Recessive	x	Normal/Recessive	=	Normal/Recessive Cocks, Recessive Cocks, Normal/Recessive Hens, Recessive Hens
(Reverse Pairing gives same expectations)				
Recessive	x	Recessive	=	Recessive Cocks, Recessive Hens

Dominant Mutation Chart

Dominant (SF)	x	Normal	=	Normal Cocks, Dominant (SF) Cocks, Normal Hens, Dominant (SF) Hens
(Reverse Pairing gives same expectations)				
Dominant (SF)	x	Dominant (SF)	=	Normal Cocks, Dominant (SF) Cocks, Dominant (DF) Cocks, Normal Hens, Dominant (SF) Hens, Dominant (DF) Hens
Dominant (SF)	x	Dominant (DF)	=	Dominant (SF) Cocks, Dominant (DF) Cocks, Dominant (SF) Hens, Dominant (DF) Hens
(Reverse Pairing gives same expectations)				
Dominant (DF)	x	Normal	=	Dominant (SF) Cocks, Dominant (SF) Hens
(Reverse Pairing gives same expectations)				
Dominant (DF)	x	Dominant (DF)	=	Dominant (DF) Cocks, Dominant (DF) Hens

SPONTANEOUS SPORTS

Mutated colour forms appear from time to time through spontaneous sports and, unless these are preserved by correct matings, they can disappear as quickly as they came. Some understanding of genetics will certainly increase our ability to perpetuate mutations through these chance arrivals by enabling us to discover the mode of inheritance. This is secondary to establishing the colour form and follows through from the elimination of inheritance modes one at a time.

Silver-satinette greenfinch mule

Dominant Mutations

These are the easiest to establish, since a visual colour form of this mutation is capable of producing its own likeness in the first generation, irrespective of its sex and without any inbreeding.

When you are breeding dominants the colour form is visual and cannot be carried by a normal in hidden form (generally known as a split form). New colour forms that are dominant mutations can turn up as spontaneous sports at any time, male or female, but they are always in what is known as 'single-factor' form, an incomplete dominant. As will be seen from the chart, when one of these is paired to a normal, half of the progeny are of the mutation colour. However, when two single factors of the mutation are paired together they produce young of which 25% are of normal colour and 75% of the mutated colour. Of the mutated young, 25% will receive a double dose of the factor producing the mutation (known as 'double-factor') and they may be visually different (in a dilute factor, much paler) or appear the same. double-factor forms of the mutation are fully dominant and, when paired to normals, produce all mutation young of the single-factor type. So it will be seen that dominant mutations are not only the easiest to establish but also lend themselves to improvements in exhibition qualities when paired to good exhibition-type normals.

Recessive Sex-linked Mutations

These are not so easy to establish. Although the rules governing sex-linked inheritance are quite straight-forward it is important to remember that the results from pairing a sex-linked cock of a mutated colour form to a normal hen are quite different from those obtained from pairing a normal-coloured cock to a sex-linked mutation hen. The reason for this is that a cock can be either pure normal or a visual normal bird with the ability to pass on the colour mutation to some of his young (referred to as a 'carrier' or 'split') or of a visual mutated colour form; whereas a hen can only be a normal-coloured bird or a visual colour mutation. In other words, a normal-coloured hen cannot be split for the sex-linked mutation; she is what you see. Unfortunately there is no significant visual difference between a normal cock and a visual normal cock carrying the mutation factor, so its true genetic make-up can only be proven through test matings. However, as can be seen from the chart, certain matings produce visual normal cocks guaranteed to be carriers of the mutation.

When a sex-linked colour mutation turns up, the first bird of the visual mutated form is always a hen. If such a hen is paired to a normal colour cock all the young produced, both cocks and hens, will be of normal colour, but all the young cocks, although of normal appearance, will carry the new colour. If these young cocks are paired to normal hens, 25% of the young produced will be of the mutation colour. Because of the mode of inheritance these will all be hens, and normal hens will also be produced. All the young cocks produced will be visual normals, half of them pure normal and the other half carriers of the mutation colour. These young cocks would need to be test-mated to find out which are carrying the mutated gene.

It follows that, to establish the new colour in the shortest possible time, we need to obtain a new-colour cock. To do this we must resort to inbreeding, pairing a new-colour hen to either her father or one of her sons: a practice which should not be taken too far because it can lead to infertility, dead-in-shell or deformed and weak chicks. Once the new-colour cock has been produced it can be paired to an unrelated normal hen. All the young hens of the pairing will then be of the mutated colour and all the young cocks will be of normal appearance but carrying the mutation. These are called 'carriers' or 'splits' and shown as 'normal/mutation' on the tables. When sufficient distantly-related cocks and hens of the new colour are produced they can be paired together to give a clutch in which all the young, cocks and hens, are of the new mutated colour form.

Recessive Autosomal Mutations

Because of their mode of inheritance, these can be difficult to establish. Inbreeding is necessary at first to establish these colour forms, which can lead to problems, particularly in the early stages. Patience and perseverance are essential to see these colour forms fully established. It is important to remember that, unlike the dominants and sex-linked mutations, splits occur in both cocks and hens.

It is also important to realise that the mutation must be present in both parents before visual examples can be produced. Recessive mutations can be carried for many generations in hidden split form but, when two splits come together, the visual form of the mutation will be produced. These can be either cocks or hens. It will then be necessary to pair these back to the opposite-sex parent. Such a pairing will produce more of the mutation in visual form and all the non-visual young produced will be carriers of the mutation.

The above route will achieve results in the shortest possible time. Unfortunately such close pairings often produce weak and sickly mutation young. In the long term it would be better to outcross with the visual mutation by pairing it to one, two or more unrelated normals. This pairing, although not producing any visual forms of the mutation, would produce all young split for the mutation. You can then pair these more distantly related birds together, split x split, producing much stronger young of the new mutated colour form and thus ensuring a better chance of the survival and establishment of the mutation.

GREENFINCH COLOUR MUTATIONS

The colour of the normal greenfinch is made up of the same pigments as the canary, though they are distributed in a slightly different way, giving the species its own individual appearance. The lipochrome pigment forms the basic ground colour and the melanin pigments overlay the ground colour. As far as is known, the melanin pigments in the greenfinch consist of one black and two brown. The first two are known as eumelanin black and eumelanin brown, both of which are situated on the inner webbing of the feather. The second

Pair cinnamon pied greenfinch (Right: hen, Left: cock)

brown melanin is known as phaeomelanin and is situated on the outer webbing of the feather. The lipochrome pigment (yellow in the greenfinch) with the melanin pigments make up what is seen as the normal greenfinch, as yellow mixed with black makes green. Different distribution of these pigments, particularly of the lipochrome and eumelanin black, gives the male and female of the species a different appearance. This is known as dimorphism and is clearly seen in all greenfinch mutations established so far.

Cinnamon

A sex-linked mutation, this is the first greenfinch mutation to be established. Cinnamons are recorded in many old published works as unusual sightings in wild flocks. However, they did not become established in domestic bred stocks until the 1950s, when pioneer colour enthusiasts such as A H Scott of Fordingham built up stocks of these birds. In this mutation the eumelanin black is completely suppressed, removed or changed to brown, but the eumelanin brown, phaeo melanin and lipochrome pigments are retained, giving us a rich golden cinnamon brown bird. It has pink eyes when hatched, but these darken at a few days old as melanin pigments develop. Since it is sex-linked the following expectations apply:

Visual Normal/Cinnamon	x	Normal	= Normal Cocks, Visual Normal/Cinnamon Cocks, Normal Hens, Cinnamon Hens
Normal	x	Cinnamon	= Visual Normal/Cinnamon Cocks, Normal Hens
Visual Normal/Cinnamon	x	Cinnamon	= Visual Normal/Cinnamon Cocks, Cinnamon Cocks, Normal Hens, Cinnamon Hens
Cinnamon	x	Normal	= Visual Normal/Cinnamon Cocks, Cinnamon Hens
Cinnamon	x	Cinnamon	= Cinnamon Cocks, Cinnamon Hens

Lutino

This is again sex-linked in its mode of inheritance and is the second greenfinch mutation to be established. Early sightings of these birds in wild flocks are recorded but they did not become fully established in domestic bred stocks until the 1960s. Syd Evans of Port Talbot recorded the first lutino cock to be bred and, with others, was responsible for much of the work in establishing this mutation. Much discussion has taken place since then as to whether these birds are true lutinos (that is, a sex-linked ino mutation of the normal greenfinch), and several theories have been put forward. However, lutino is the name given, and will no doubt remain, since there are many other species, such as budgerigar, cockatiel, and lovebird, in which this red-eyed, sex-linked mutation has occurred and been called 'lutino'. To date, it is only in the canary that this sex-linked form of ino is given a different name (satinette). One reason for this appears to be that, for the lutino breeder, perfection is a bird that is, as near as possible, devoid of melanin pigments or suffusions of such pigments; for the breeder of satinettes, perfection is a bird clearly showing melanin pigments in a dilute or suffused form.

In the lutino greenfinch all melanin pigments are suppressed, giving a red-eyed bird of a clear yellow appearance, but in many some diffusion is detectable, depending on how they are produced. When paired to normal the following expectations apply:

Visual Normal/Lutino	x	Normal	= Normal Cocks, Visual Normal/Lutino Cocks, Normal Hens, Lutino Hens
Normal	x	Lutino	= Visual Normal/Lutino Cocks, Normal Hens
Visual Normal/Lutino	x	Lutino	= Visual Normal/Lutino Cocks, Lutino Cocks, Normal Hens, Lutino Hens

Lutino	x Normal	= Visual Normal/Lutino Cocks, Lutino Hens
Lutino	x Lutino	= Lutino Cocks, Lutino Hens

Cinnamon-Ino (Satinette)

Early experimental pairings of lutino to cinnamon and vice versa showed it was not possible at this stage to have a lutino carrying the cinnamon factor or a cinnamon carrying the lutino factor:

Lutino	x	Cinnamon	=	Visual Normal/Cinnamon/Lutino Cocks, Lutino Hens
Cinnamon	x	Lutino	=	Visual Normal/Cinnamon/Lutino Cocks, Cinnamon Hens

However, it was found that these double-split cocks (cocks carrying the two mutation colours), when paired back, gave interesting results. It will be seen from the pairings below that it was now possible in theory to produce lutino carrying cinnamon and vice versa but, since a visual cinnamon cannot carry the factor for normal, and lutino is a normal version of ino, he should only be described as cinnamon/ino. In practice, such birds would have been difficult to identify at this stage. Few experiments, as far as we are aware, were recorded or concluded on the latter pairings, since it was possible to achieve positive results through more straightforward pairings.

Visual Normal/Cinnamon/Lutino	x Normal	=	Normal Cocks, Visual Normal/Lutino Cocks, Visual Normal/Cinnamon Cocks, Visual Normal/Cinnamon/Lutino Cocks, Normal Hens, Cinnamon Hens, Lutino Hens, Cinnamon-Ino Hens
Visual Normal/Cinnamon/Lutino	x Cinnamon	=	Visual Normal/Cinnamon Cocks, Visual Normal/Cinnamon/Lutino Cocks, Cinnamon Cocks, Cinnamon/Ino Cocks, Normal Hens, Cinnamon Hens, Lutino Hens, Cinnamon-Ino Hens
Visual Normal/Cinnamon/Lutino	x Lutino	=	Visual Normal/Lutino Cocks, Visual Normal/Cinnamon/Lutino Cocks, Lutino Cocks, Lutino/Cinnamon Cocks, Normal Hens, Lutino Hens, Cinnamon Hens, Cinnamon-Ino Hens
Lutino/Cinnamon	x Lutino	=	Lutino Cocks, Lutino/Cinnamon Cocks, Lutino Hens, Cinnamon-Ino Hens
Lutino/Cinnamon	x Cinnamon	=	Visual Normal/Cinnamon/Lutino Cocks, Cinnamon/Ino Cocks, Lutino Hens, Cinnamon-Ino Hens
Cinnamon/Ino	x Lutino	=	Visual Normal/Cinnamon/Lutino Cocks, Lutino/Cinnamon Cocks, Cinnamon Hens, Cinnamon-Ino Hens
Cinnamon/Ino	x Cinnamon	=	Cinnamon Cocks, Cinnamon/Ino Cocks, Cinnamon Hens, Cinnamon-Ino Hens

The cinnamon-ino hens produced are a combination or composite bird, derived from a crossover and the result of a fusing together of the two mutated genes, cinnamon and lutino. Undoubtedly the first of these was produced by accident. Bob Partridge, along with others, carried out experiments with the intention of producing these birds and was the first to record a cock of the combination colour. Experimental pairings were backed up by fellow colour enthusiasts. It was found that, for some inexplicable reason, these combination colour variants retained much of the brown melanins, giving a yellow bird with dilute cinnamon suffusion laced throughout, even to the extent of making the eyes a darker ruby-red.

Because these birds closely resembled the brown satinette canary they became known as satinette greenfinches. By pairing cinnamon cocks to these satinette hens it was possible to obtain cinnamon cocks guaranteed to be carrying the ino factor. These split cocks, paired back to satinette hens, produced the satinettes in both sexes. Such pairings also proved that the satinette was in fact the cinnamon (brown) version of the ino mutation.

Cinnamon	x	Satinette	=	Cinnamon/Satinette Cocks, Cinnamon Hens
Cinnamon/Satinette	x	Satinette	=	Cinnamon/Satinette Cocks, Satinette Cocks,
				Cinnamon Hens, Satinette Hens
Satinette	x	Cinnamon	=	Cinnamon/Satinette Cocks, Satinette Hens
Satinette	x	Satinette	=	Satinette Cocks, Satinette Hens

Other pairings to produce satinettes can be used but are not recommended since, generally, the satinettes produced will be of inferior colour or cause the crossover process to be reversed:

Normal	x	Satinette	=	Visual Normal/Satinette Cocks, Normal Hens
Satinette	x	Normal	=	Visual Normal/Satinette Cocks, Satinette Hens
Visual Normal/Satinette	x	Normal	=	Visual Normal Cocks, Visual Normal/Cinnamon Cocks,
				Visual Normal/Lutino Cocks,
				Visual Normal/Satinette Cocks, Normal Hens,
				Cinnamon Hens, Lutino Hens, Satinette Hens
Visual Normal/Satinette	x	Satinette	=	Visual Normal/Satinette Cocks, Lutino/Cinnamon Cocks,
				Cinnamon/Ino Cocks, Satinette Cocks, Normal Hens,
				Lutino Hens, Cinnamon Hens, Satinette Hens
Lutino	x	Satinette	=	Lutino/Cinnamon Cocks, Lutino Hens
Satinette	x	Lutino	=	Lutino/Cinnamon Cocks, Satinette Hens
Lutino/Cinnamon	x	Satinette	=	Lutino/Cinnamon Cocks, Satinette Cocks, Lutino Hens,
				Satinette Hens

Although the term Satinette is used in many of the pairings above for ease of understanding, it should be remembered that the term is not technically correct. A greenfinch described as visual normal/satinette is the same as visual normal/cinnamon/lutino. Cinnamon/satinette is the same as cinnamon/ino and lutino/satinette is the same as lutino/cinnamon. This explains why certain pairings appear to cause the crossover process to revert. The above principle will apply to many other pairings in which the composite varieties are used.

Silver Mutation

These greyish-coloured dilutes began to appear in domestic-bred stocks around the 1950s and were recorded by the early enthusiasts A H Scott, Syd Evans and others. Later, conflicting reports caused some confusion, some breeders stating that these dilutes had dark eyes like normals, others that they had pink eyes like cinnamons. In fact they were breeding two separate varieties: a normal dilute with dark eyes (agate) and a very similar dilute with pink eyes (pastel), both of which were sex-linked in their inheritance patterns. Unfortunately, only a few breeders, mainly in the East Anglian region, persisted with these dilutes, so stocks were scarce, and were to remain so throughout the 1950s and 1960s.

In the early 1970s Bob Partridge imported a small number of these dilutes from Belgian breeders. Although all the birds looked very similar, when they were bred from it soon became apparent that the importation had contained both types of these dilute varieties. They bred exceptionally well and a number were passed to fellow colour breeders. These were supplemented in the 1980s by other small imports by

Cinnamon greenfinch pair (Left: hen, Right: cock)

Roger Caton and others, causing these birds to become fully established throughout the UK. It soon became apparent that not only were these varieties closely linked but they had occurred on the same mutated gene as the lutino and were multiple alleles. Since the dark-eyed agate mutation, although sex-linked, is dominant to both pastel and sex-linked ino varieties, we will discuss the agate first:

The Agate Greenfinch: In this mutation all the melanin pigments are subtly and evenly diluted, allowing the lipochrome ground colour to show through the melanin, particularly in the colour point areas of forehead, upper breast, wing butts, lower abdomen and rump. The cock of this mutation therefore has a lime green appearance, overlaid with grey. The hen is much greyier, but still shows good lipochrome colour point areas of highbrow line, upper breast wingbutts and rump. When paired to normal and cinnamon, expectations are:

Normal	x	Agate	=	Visual Normal/Agate Cocks, Normal Hens
Visual Normal/Agate	x	Normal	=	Normal Cocks, Visual Normal/Agate Cocks, Normal Hens, Agate Hens
Visual Normal/Agate	x	Agate	=	Visual Normal/Agate Cocks, Agate Cocks, Normal Hens, Agate Hens
Agate	x	Normal	=	Visual Normal/Agate Cocks, Agate Hens
Agate	x	Agate	=	Agate Cocks, Agate Hens
Visual Normal/Agate	x	Cinnamon	=	Visual Normal/Cinnamon Cocks, Visual Normal/Cinnamon/Agate Cocks, Normal Hens, Agate Hens
Cinnamon	x	Agate	=	Visual Normal/Cinnamon/Agate Cocks, Cinnamon Hens
Agate	x	Cinnamon	=	Visual Normal/Cinnamon/Agate Cocks, Agate Hens
Visual Normal/Cinnamon	x	Agate	=	Visual Normal/Agate Cocks, Visual Normal/Cinnamon/Agate Cocks, Normal Hens, Cinnamon Hens
Visual Normal/Cinnamon/Agate	x	Normal	=	Normal Cocks, Visual Normal/Cinnamon Cocks, Visual Normal/Agate Cocks, Visual Normal/Cinnamon/Agate Cocks, Normal Hens, Cinnamon Hens, Agate Hens, Isabel Hens (Cinnamon-Dilute)
Visual Normal/Cinnamon/Agate	x	Cinnamon	=	Visual Normal/Cinnamon Cocks, Visual Normal/Cinnamon/Agate Cocks, Cinnamon Cocks, Cinnamon/Agate Cocks, Normal Hens, Cinnamon Hens, Agate Hens, Isabel Hens (Cinnamon-Dilute)
Visual Normal/Cinnamon/Agate	x	Agate	=	Visual Normal/Agate Cocks, Visual Normal/Cinnamon/Agate Cocks, Agate Cocks, Agate/Cinnamon Cocks, Normal Hens, CinnamonHens, Agate Hens, Isabel Hens (Cinnamon-Dilute)
Normal	x	Isabel	=	Visual Normal/Isabel Cocks, Normal Hens
Cinnamon	x	Isabel	=	Cinnamon/Isabel Cocks, Cinnamon Hens
Agate	x	Isabel	=	Agate/Isabel Cocks, Agate Hens

Visual Normal/Isabel	x	Isabel	=	Visual Normal/Isabel Cocks, Cinnamon/Isabel Cocks, Agate/Isabel Cocks, Isabel Cocks, Normal Hens, Cinnamon Hens, Agate Hens, Isabel Hens
Cinnamon/Isabel	x	Isabel	=	Cinnamon/Isabel Cocks, Isabel Cocks, Cinnamon Hens, Isabel Hens
Agate/Isabel	x	Isabel	=	Agate/Isabel Cocks, Isabel Cocks, Agate Hens, Isabel Hens
Isabel	x	Normal	=	Visual Normal/Isabel Cocks, Isabel Hens
Isabel	x	Cinnamon	=	Cinnamon/Isabel Cocks, Isabel Hens
Isabel	x	Isabel	=	Isabel Cocks, Isabel Hens

As will be seen in the above pairings, agate x cinnamon and vice versa produce visual normal double-split cocks, which in turn can be used to produce the composite cinnamon-dilute. This colour variety is known as the Isabel. As with the normal-dilute version of the mutation, all melanin pigment is diluted evenly, allowing the ground colour to show through and giving a bird of a pale cinnamon shade, still showing yellow at all colour points.

When we pair a dilute (agate or Isabel) to an ino (lutino or satinette) we see that the pattern of inheritance changes and the dilute factor becomes dominant to the ino factor:

Visual Normal/Lutino	x	Agate	=	Visual Normal/Agate Cocks, Visual Normal/Agate/Lutino Cocks, Agate Cocks, Agate/Lutino Cocks, Normal Hens, Lutino Hens
Visual Normal/Agate	x	Lutino	=	Visual Normal/Lutino Cocks, Visual Normal/Lutino/Agate Cocks, Agate/Lutino Cocks, Normal Hens, Agate Hens
Agate	x	Lutino	=	Agate/Lutino Cocks, Agate Hens
Lutino	x	Agate	=	Agate/Lutino Cocks, Lutino Hens
Agate/Lutino	x	Agate	=	Agate Cocks, Agate/Lutino Cocks, Agate Hens, Lutino Hens *
Agate/Lutino	x	Lutino	=	Agate/Lutino Cocks, Lutino Cocks, Agate Hens, Lutino Hens*
Visual Normal/Satinette	x	Agate	=	Visual Normal/Agate Cocks, Visual Normal/Cinnamon/Agate Cocks, Visual Normal/Lutino/Agate. Cocks, Visual Normal/Satinette/Agate Cocks, Agate Cocks, Agate/Cinnamon Cocks, Agate/Lutino Cocks, Agate/Satinette Cocks, Normal Hens, Cinnamon Hens, Lutino Hens, Satinette Hens
Agate/Satinette	x	Lutino	=	Agate/Lutino Cocks, Agate/Satinette Cocks, Lutino Cocks, Lutino/Satinette Cocks, Agate Hens, Isabel Hens, Lutino Hens*, Satinette Hens*
Agate/Satinette	x	Agate	=	Agate Cocks, Agate/Cinnamon Cocks, Agate/Lutino Cocks, Agate/Satinette Cocks, Agate Hens, Isabel Hens, Lutino Hens*, Satinette Hens
Agate	x	Satinette	=	Agate/Satinette Cocks, Agate Hens
Satinette	x	Agate	=	Agate/Satinette Cocks, Satinette Hens

Agate/Satinette	x	Satinette	=	Agate/Satinette Cocks, Satinette Cocks, Agate Hens, Satinette Hens*
Visual Normal/Isabel	x	Lutino	=	Visual Normal/Lutino Cocks, Visual Normal/Lutino/Agate Cocks, Visual Normal/Lutino/Cinnamon Cocks, Visual Normal/Lutino/Isabel Cocks, Agate/Lutino Cocks, Agate/Lutino/Cinnamon Cocks, Normal Hens, Agate Hens, Cinnamon Hens, Isabel Hens
Visual Normal/Lutino	x	Isabel	=	Visual Normal/Isabel Cocks, Visual Normal/Isabel/Lutino Cocks, Agate/Isabel Cocks, Agate/Isabel/Lutino Cocks, Normal Hens, Lutino Hens
Isabel	x	Lutino	=	Agate/Lutino/Isabel Cocks, Isabel Hens
Lutino	x	Isabel	=	Agate/Isabel/Lutino Cocks, Lutino Hens
Agate/Lutino	x	Isabel	=	Agate/Isabel Cocks, Agate/Isabel/Lutino Cocks, Agate Hens, Lutino Hens*
Agate/Isabel	x	Lutino	=	Agate/Lutino Cocks, Agate/Lutino/Isabel Cocks, Agate Hens, Isabel Hens
Isabel	x	Satinette	=	Isabel/Satinette Cocks, Isabel Hens
Satinette	x	Isabel	=	Isabel/Satinette Cocks, Satinette Hens
Isabel/Satinette	x	Satinette	=	Isabel/Satinette Cocks, Satinette Cocks, Isabel Hens, Satinette Hens*
Visual Normal/Isabel	x	Satinette	=	Visual Normal/Satinette Cocks, Visual Normal/Satinette/Isabel Cocks, Agate/Satinette Cocks, Agate/Satinette/Isabel/ Cocks, Isabel/Satinette Cocks, Normal Hens, Agate Hens, Cinnamon Hens, Isabel Hens
Agate/Isabel	x	Satinette	=	Agate/Satinette Cocks, Isabel/Satinette Cocks, Agate Hens, Isabel Hens
Visual Normal/Satinette	x	Isabel	=	VisualNormal/Isabel Cocks, Visual Normal/Isabel/Ino Cocks, Cinnamon/Isabel Cocks, Cinnamon/Isabel/Ino Cocks, Agate/Cinnamon Cocks, Agate/Cinnamon/Ino Cocks, Isabel/Ino Cocks, Normal Hens, Cinnamon Hens, Lutino Hens, Agate Hens, Satinette Hens

The appearance of the birds marked with an asterisk (*) caused considerable debate on nomenclature. Should these visual lutino and visual satinette birds be described as agate-ino and Isabel-ino respectively? Experiments so far have not proved them any different to a lutino or satinette. No doubt the debate will continue.

The Pastel Greenfinch: The origin of this variety is open to debate. Is it a mutation in its own right or was it the result of a crossover between the agate and ino factors? Certainly when we study the previous matings we see that we have produced birds capable of giving us a crossover. Did the two colours fuse together? If so, because the agate factor dominates, the ino factor could be rendered unable to express itself fully, but still able to dilute the agate further, giving us a bird visually similar to the agate, but with pink eyes that darken like those of the cinnamon within a few days of hatching. We know the agate and lutino mutations have occurred on the same gene and we know a crossover, though difficult, is possible. It is known that, when two such closely-linked mutations fuse together, separation is extremely difficult and almost impossible. On the other hand, a crossover between these two mutations (the agate-ino) should appear indistinguishable from a lutino. We know that there were reports of these pink-eyed dilutes well before the lutino became fully established. We also know that the agate greenfinch is the same mutated form as the agate canary, and the lutino greenfinch is the same as the satinette canary, and of similar appearance. However, the agate-satinette canary does not look like the pink-eyed dilute greenfinch. In the agate-satinette canary the satinette factor expresses itself as we would expect.

Whether the pastel greenfinch is the result of a crossover or a mutation in its own right, we know it breeds true, and that it has occurred on the same gene as the lutino and agate.

The normal pastel generally has much more grey suffusion than the agate, giving it a light ash-grey colouration. This grey suffusion to some extent masks the lipochrome yellow, so the bird generally lacks the bright yellow ground colour. This applies to both sexes in both normal and brown series birds. The normal (green) series bird normal pastel is referred to as 'pastel' and the (cinnamon) brown series bird is referred to as 'brown-pastel'. When paired to (green series) normal and lutino or (brown series) cinnamon and satinette it will follow exactly the same mode of inheritance as the agate, being recessive sex-linked to normal and cinnamon but dominant to lutino and satinette. This means that, by replacing the term agate with pastel and Isabel with brown-pastel, expectations can easily be worked out:

Pastel	x Normal	=	Visual Normal/Pastel Cocks, Pastel Hens
Brown-Pastel	x Cinnamon	=	Cinnamon/brown-pastel Cocks, Brown-pastel Hens
Pastel	x Lutino	=	Pastel/Lutino Cocks, Pastel Hens
Brown-Pastel	x Satinette	=	Brown-Pastel/Satinette Cocks, Brown-Pastel Hens

When we pair agate to pastel we find the agate is dominant to pastel so all young produced are dilute and the same will apply in the brown series.

Agate	x Pastel	=	Agate/Pastel Cocks, Agate Hens
Pastel	x Agate	=	Agate/Pastel Cocks, Pastel Hens
Agate/Pastel	x Agate	=	Agate Cocks, Agate/Pastel Cocks, Agate Hens, Pastel Hens
Agate/Pastel	x Pastel	=	Agate/Pastel Cocks, Pastel Cocks, Agate Hens, Pastel Hens
Agate/Pastel	x Normal	=	Visual Normal/Agate Cocks, Visual Normal/Agate/Pastel Cocks, Agate Hens, Pastel Hens
Isabel	x Brown-Pastel	=	Isabel/Brown-Pastel Cocks, Isabel Hens
Brown-Pastel	x Isabel	=	Isabel/Brown-Pastel Cocks, Brown-Pastel Hens
Isabel/Brown-Pastel	x Isabel	=	Isabel Cocks, Isabel/Brown-Pastel Cocks, Isabel Hens, Brown-Pastel Hens
Isabel/Brown-Pastel	x Brown-Pastel	=	Isabel/Brown-Pastel Cocks, Brown-Pastel Cocks, Isabel Hens, Brown-Pastel Hens
Isabel/Brown-Pastel	x Cinnamon	=	Cinnamon/Isabel Cocks, Cinnamon/Isabel/Brown-Pastel Cocks, Isabel Hens, Brown-Pastel Hens

As you can see, once again we produce birds capable of producing composite varieties: visual normal/agate/pastel and visual cinnamon/Isabel/brown-pastel, birds of intermediate colouration, the agate-pastel and its brown counterpart the Isabel-pastel.

Although all possible pairings have not been listed, we have tried to cover most of them, giving some idea of their complexity. Because of variations in colour shades within a mutation and the effects of cross-colour pairings (covered later), positive identifications of each variety within this group are very difficult and almost impossible once past the fledgling stage. Breeders, however, can positively identify each variety by noting and recording eye colouration soon after hatching. A resumé of the group is given for guidance:

Brown-pastel greenfinch (hen)

Normal (green) series:

Agate	-	Eyes are dark as in normal when the bird hatches and remain so.
Pastel	-	Eyes are pink as in cinnamon when the bird hatches, darkening to normal appearance at between three and seven days old.
Agate-Pastel	-	Eyes are damson-coloured when the bird hatches, darkening to normal appearance at between three and five days.

Brown (cinnamon series):

Isabel	-	Eyes are pink as in cinnamon when the bird hatches, darkening to normal appearance at three to seven days old.
Brown-Pastel	-	Eyes are red when hatched and only darken slowly, the bird fledging with and retaining dark ruby eye colouration.
Isabel-Pastel	-	Eyes are pink, similar to but lighter than a cinnamon, on hatching, slowly darkening to a normal appearance at fledging.

The Pied (Variegated) Greenfinch

Although over the years there have been regular reports of pied or variegated greenfinches, the vast majority proved to be non-genetic and incapable of producing their own likeness. The few which showed promise genetically only produced the odd specimen before fate took a hand, making sure they were not established at that time. However, the long-awaited breakthrough finally came in the 1980s.

In 1987, Bill Roberts of New York in Lincolnshire was put in touch with Bob Partridge concerning some unusual coloured greenfinches. This led to photographs of the birds being presented and Bob Partridge agreeing to make a visit to examine the birds. Several of these birds were indeed pieds, ranging from those exhibiting only a single non-melanin feather to those showing as much as 75% non-melanin areas. Mr Roberts explained that in 1984 he paired a cinnamon cock to two normal hens with the intention of producing a line of cinnamons. These, as expected, produced visual normal cocks carrying the cinnamon factor and cinnamon hens, and these were inter-mated for the following two seasons without the introduction of any new stock. It was then he noticed some of the young were of what he described as 'of a lightish appearance'. These were birds in which the melanin pigments had been removed or suppressed in the areas of the lower abdomen and flanks, allowing the lipochrome ground colour to show through.

Feeling that this feature may be worth 'fixing', he paired birds showing this light suffusion together. Among the resulting youngsters were a number of these birds of light suffusion, but also a number of pieds. Mr Roberts felt that, because of his age (he was in his seventies at the time), he would not be able to carry out the necessary experimental matings required to verify the genetics of these birds and secure the mutation for the future. He did not wish to see them go the way of predecessors and die out, so an exchange of mutation stocks to our mutual benefit was agreed and, in 1988, Bob Partridge began to establish the mutation and its genetic pattern. It was not easy, as stocks were now inbred. Matings were carried out and stock built up to enable some to be passed to other enthusiasts. Over the next five years the mutation was established.

It proved to be a recessive autosomal mutation of deep recessive character, the variegation factor being unstable, so producing birds with considerable areas of variegation was a long process. Head, tail and wing marked birds and splits produced from these produced birds of similar marking, together with the occasional variegated bird. These variegated birds produced a much higher percentage of variegateds when paired to other variegateds, but when paired to non-pieds the splits produced tended to produce mainly head, wing and tail marked young. However, if paired to variegateds the numbers of variegated young produced increased again. If the process of pairing variegated x variegated is continued, light variegated birds and, ultimately, tick marked and even clear are produced.

The mutation proved to be the same as that which produced the variegated canary. This was proved through test matings, using split pied greenfinches to variegated canaries. These matings produced a high percentage of variegated greenfinch x canary hybrids and provided a useful means of test-mating numbers of the possible splits being produced at the time.

In 1989, Mrs Angela Titmus of Retford in Nottinghamshire contacted Bob Partridge to report that she had produced a number of pieds during the 1989 season from a pair of greenfinches consisting of a visual normal cock and a cinnamon hen. These had come from different sources and were, as far as is known, completely unrelated, and there did not appear to be a connection with the Lincolnshire line, although neither possibility could be completely ruled out.

The birds showed similar variegation to the original Lincolnshire pied, being head, wing and tail marked, and some having the odd splash on the back or abdomen. However, they did not have the yellow suffused areas of the Lincolnshire line, the areas of variegation having a more abrupt line of demarcation. Mrs Titmus was able to keep this line going by inbreeding with some pairs and outcrossing others.

In 1992, Bob Partridge paired one of the Nottingham birds, a head, wing and tail marked cinnamon cock, to one of his variegated cinnamon pied hens. This pair produced all pieds but one, the odd one out being a cinnamon cock which, although showing no variegation, did have a suffused lower abdomen. A hen of the Nottingham line was then paired to a variegated canary cock, which produced three mules, all variegated. The pairings carried out so far with these Nottingham birds, though not conclusive, suggest that, whether or not these two lines originated from a single source, they are probably of a singular recessive pied mutation. Since the pied greenfinch is of recessive genetic form, its expectations can easily be worked out from the recessive autosomal chart shown previously.

The pied mutation is recessive to all the previously established colour mutations of the greenfinch and the processes of producing pieds of these mutations will all follow the same pattern. It is only necessary to change the nomenclature used: to work out expectations in normal pieds, replace the word 'recessive' with 'normal' pied in the recessive chart.

To transfer the pied factor to other colours is a comparatively easy task, but will take more than one season to achieve. For example, if we wish to produce agate-pieds using a nucleus of normal pied x agate pairings, this will produce all visual normal young. The visual normal cocks produced will carry both agate and pied factors, but the visual normal hens will only carry the pied factor. By pairing these visual normal/agate/pied cocks to pied or split pied hens we can produce a percentage of agate-pied hens. Agate or split agate cocks can then be paired to these agate-pied hens, producing agate cocks and agate hens, all of which will carry the pied factor (agate/pied). Agate/pied x Agate-pied or Agate/pied x Agate/pied will produce a percentage of agate-pieds in both sexes. The same procedure can be used to produce pieds in all the established mutations of the greenfinch.

Other Colour Variations

Other colour variation produced in the greenfinch include slate blues and blacks, but these have not been established to date, as all young seem to have proved to be non-genetic forms. Hopefully, the next long-awaited breakthrough in this species will be in a form that will change the lipochrome yellow to white or ivory, giving us a whole new range of exciting colour variants.

Effects of Cross-Colour Pairings

Unless you have some specific purpose in mind, inter-pairing of the different colour mutations is not recommended. Although it is possible to produce good quality birds from such pairings, very few will be of high exhibition standard. The exception to this is the cinnamon, which can be used instead of normal with no

Satinette greenfinch (hen)

ill effects on colour. In fact, it may be used to advantage in certain matings, assuming the cinnamon concerned is of the correct colour to start with. This would apply even when using a normal colour. Correct colour is a most important feature of all colour mutations, though markings, type and size will also need to be given due consideration if exhibition is the aim.

The use of the ino factor (lutino and satinette) will have a detrimental effect on other colours, including normal, as it can introduce a mealy, smoky or washed-out appearance. It can however be used to advantage in production of the agate-pastel and Isabel-pastel composite varieties. It is not a good idea to use the ino factor in the production of good-quality exhibition agates and pastels or their brown counterparts, the Isabel and brown-pastel, as they generally produce inferior colour in such varieties.

Cross-colour pairing has been one of the main causes of problems in identification of some of the dilute varieties. For this reason, cross-pairing of agate and pastel with each other should be avoided. All the dilute factors (ino, agate and pastel in both normal and brown series) affect the colour of their progeny when used in cross-colour pairings. Possibly a few example pairings would give a better picture. If we mate a cinnamon cock of good colour and type to a satinette, Isabel, brown-pastel or Isabel-pastel hen, with a view to improving that variety, all the resulting young from such a pairing will be visual cinnamon. The cocks will be carriers of whatever mutation hen is used. However, the vast majority of the progeny will not compare in purity or depth of colour to the cock used. In fact, most of them will be of a washed out or milky cinnamon colour. The cocks will be very useful in the further production of the mutation colour they carry but should not be used in the further production of cinnamon; they will soon ruin a good line of cinnamons. Caution must also be used in the use of the cinnamon hens produced for, although they are genetically pure cinnamon, their inferior colour will be just as harmful and should not be used for pure cinnamon production; again, they can be usefully employed in the production of the dilute varieties.

The same would apply if we used a normal instead of cinnamon in the mating, or a normal to lutino, agate, pastel or agate-pastel. Though the colour expectations would be different, the principle is the same. Other examples would be agate x lutino or satinette, producing all dark-eyed dilute agate young that are pale or washed-out in colour. Pastel x lutino or satinette produces all pink-eyed dilute pastel young that, again, are pale or washed-out in colour.

In these matings the visual effect is similar to, though not as obvious as, that obtained when using some dominant double-factor dilute mutations in other species, although we are using sex-inked, single-factor, multiple-allele, dilutes. As suggested earlier, this double-factor effect can be put to good use in the production of the composite dilute agate-pastel and Isabel-pastel. By pairing these combination dilutes to lutino or satinette we can obtain the maximum effect within these composite dilute varieties.

So far, the effects of the pied mutation on other colours are still at the experimental stage. However, caution will be required: once it is introduced into a line of a self-coloured mutation, good birds spoilt by the appearance of the odd non-pigmented feather will occur with increasing frequency. The lutino is the exception since any variegation would effectively be masked by the ino factor, rendering it possible to produce good visual lutino and pied birds in the same nest. There seems little to be gained from combining pied with satinette or some of the other delicate shades of composite varieties, but additions to the normal-pied in the form of cinnamon, agate and pastel are attractive. Early experiments suggest that the pied factor could be useful in the production of high-coloured agates and Isabels, since many of the self-coloured carriers of the pied mutation show very good colour at all colour points.

In conclusion: there is still much to be learnt about the effects of cross-colour pairing. Through the use of controlled experimental pairings our knowledge of cross-colour matings and their effects will continue to increase.

Chapter 10

The Law

It is beyond the scope of this volume to give a full explanation of the Wild Life and Countryside Act 1981, which is the current bird protection act; it is both long and complicated. All keepers and breeders of birds, particularly keepers and breeders of our native British birds, should acquaint themselves fully with its provisions. Copies of the act can be obtained from Her Majesty's Stationery Office. However, some of the most important points are as follows:

1   All wild birds, their nests and eggs are protected.
2   It is illegal to have any wild bird in your possession unless you have a special licence or permit to do so. A bird is only considered to be legally captive bred if its parents were legally in captivity at the time that it was hatched in a cage or aviary. If you can prove that, the bird need not be ringed; but it is recommended that whenever possible all young birds are ringed.
3   It is illegal to buy or sell a native bird except by special licence unless it is listed only on Schedule 3 Part 1 of the Wild Life and Countryside Act 1981, and then again provided that it is correctly ringed with an approved ring of the correct size. (The greenfinch is so listed.)
4   Except under special licence, only birds listed on Schedule 3 Part 1 can be exhibited, and again they must be ringed with an approved ring of the correct size.
5   It is illegal to keep or confine any bird whatsoever in a cage which is not sufficient in height, length or breadth to permit the bird to stretch its wings freely except when:
   (a)   the bird is in the course of conveyance.
   (b)   the bird is undergoing treatment by a veterinary surgeon.
   (c)   the bird is being exhibited for competition. (However, it must not remain in a show cage for more than 72 hours.)
   (d)   the bird is being trained for exhibition. (However, it must not be so confined for more than one hour in any 24-hour period.)

Tribute

Sadly Peter Lander died before the series *Popular British Birds in Aviculture* could be published.

I first met Peter in the early 1960s when he approached me for some Siberian goldfinches. The goldfinch was a species for which he had a particular fondness.

In addition to keeping and breeding birds, Peter had a keen interest in all things ornithological. I found him a quiet, unassuming man who knew his own mind. He was the driving force behind the founding of The British Bird Council, and worked tirelessly on its behalf for many years. In recent years, by his own choice, he took a back seat, but was always there when needed to give advice and a helping hand.

I worked with Peter when he compiled *British Birds in Aviculture* for the British Bird Council and felt privileged when he asked me to be co-author of the *Popular British Birds in Aviculture* series. Without Peter's initiative this series would not have been produced.

A guiding light extinguished, but memories will light our way.

Bob Partridge